MW01004696

Recovery After

Trauma Work

For Healthcare Workers

Dr. Carol Francis

Recovery After

Treating Traumas

For Healthcare Workers

Dr. Carol Francis

Title: *Recovery After Trauma Work*

Subtitle: *For Healthcare Workers*

Author: Dr. Carol Francis

Copyright 2020 by Dr. Carol Francis.

Make Life Happen Publishing * USA: Rancho Palos Verdes

Title: Recovery After Trauma Work

Subtitle: For Healthcare Workers

Original Cover Art and Interior Art by Carol Francis & All Rights Reserved for Cover and Associated Art/Marketing

ISBN: 978-1-941846-03-2

First eBbook and Paperback editions, May 2020 by Make Life Happen Publishing, Rancho Palos Verdes, CA

You Endured –

Awful devastations witnessed
Terrifying exposure to many tortuous and lonely deaths
Appallingly tough life and death decisions
Severe personal sacrifices and risks
Worrisome family needs and frightening exposures
Critical overwhelming emergencies
Disappointing lack of supports & equipment
Morally distressing dilemmas
Overwhelming demands for your time
Exhaustingly impossible need for your skills
Wreckage to multiple lives crushingly evident
Severely wailing and weeping moments of grief
Countless lifeless bodies of people you helped

You now –

Need to recover your life
Recognize the traumatic reactions you are having
Renew your personality's best qualities
Regain your health, peacefulness, vigor, and love
Regroup your friend and family connections

Recover from trauma
you have witnessed, treated, and endured.

Let me help you on your path to recovery after your
trauma work.

Thank you, Dr. Carol Francis
Clinical Psychologist

Paths to Recovery After Abuse and Trauma

Helping People Find Their Paths to Recovery and Beyond

PRIVATE ONLINE
RECOVERY EXPERIENCE

Course 10: Psychotherapies for Abuse and Trauma Recovery

Compassion Fatigue Recovery Seminar

Help for Your Health Care Giver

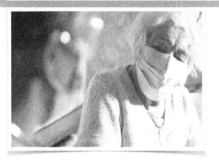

Support Your Staff's Recovery

Shift from *Compassion Fatigue* to Compassion Satisfaction

Reduce *Secondary Traumatic Stress* to Mindful Release and Ease

Replace *Professional Burnout* with Professional Enthusiasm

One-Hour Seminar for Your HealthCare Staff

(Online or OnSite Seminar conducted by Clinical Psychologist Dr. Carol Francis, 42 years of experience & author of 18 books including *Own Your Inner Peace*.)

Compassion Fatigue
Grief, Avoidance, Nightmares, Illness, Reduced Empathy

Secondary Traumatic Stress
Inconsolable, Helplessness, Fear, Flooding, Cloudy

Professional Care Giver Burnout
Irritation, Frustration, Exhaustion

1	2	3
6 TOOLS TO REDUCE	**4 TOOLS TO CREATE**	**4 TOOLS**
Compassion Fatigue	Caregiver Compassion Satisfaction	Release Stress
Secondary Trauma Stress	Caregiver Empowerment	Ease Irritation
Professional Burnout		Activate Enthusiasm

Table of Contents

Letter to Readers from Author

You do not need me to recount experiences you have endured as a trauma healthcare worker. You do not need to read descriptions about others' overwhelmingly tough moments tending to patients' crippling needs. You live those realities each hour. You share those experiences daily. You know better than anyone the horrors you have faced at work.

Instead, you deserve to have some paths
to "return" to your "new normal."
You want usable tools that you can chose to use today.
You desire healing approaches to implement now.
You need practical tactics that enhance your recovery
for the months to come.

Recovery After Trauma Work for Health Care Workers is one part of a greater program established to help you, your healthcare colleagues, and your family. You can access that ever-growing program at AbuseTraumaRecovery.com/HealthCareWorkersRecovery with informative videos, rejuvenating audios, creative exercises, respectful research blogs, and social outreach groups organized for you. You can access my team and me also through TherapyCounselingCoaching.com.

Recovery After Trauma Work helps you:

Respect and understand your style of recovery

Recognize the depths of your traumatic reactions

Restore your self-trust

Revere your personality's strengths and limits

Restore optimal healthy habits to begin healing

Rebuild inner peaceful moments for your mind, emotions, body, and spirit

Re-integrate you into daily homelife and chores, step by step

Reinvigorate your mental, physical, and emotional well-being

Reset your socializing desires and skills

Renew your relationships with family and friends

Reconsider your limitations and emotional reactions with humane regard

Recover from your work with traumatized patient and Health Care Worker's traumatic experiences

These are the 12 R's of Recovery.

Let's Begin.

Chapter 1
Your Unique Style of Recovery

Above all, respect yourself.
Do not judge yourself, please.

For many, you are a hero, perhaps an angel or saint, who dedicated yourself to helping them through dark times, dangerous times, life-threatening times.

Honor who you are: a person with essential skills, human concerns, dedication, tenacity, and endurance.

Let us thank you, sincerely, for all you have done.

I am certain that you have made mistakes you wish you could erase. You have felt like a failure when you wished you could succeed. You've been blind with exhaustion and strained beyond belief by demands you could not address. You have wanted to give up and sometimes you did. You have wanted to be invincible and realized you often were merely human.

You have memories of dreadful times, sounds of horrible situations, wailing tears for sad outcomes, and wretchedly disgusting visuals you can't seem to erase.

So please, let us thank you for your service to humans in awful moments, which most of us never glimpse in real life.

Receive Help

Since you are reading this book, or someone who loves you handed this to you, it means you need and deserve help now.

Please receive help the way your best patients did from you. Be honest about your limitations. Be clear about your needs. Be receptive to authentic interventions that match your style and your situation. Let others nurse you to your new, renewed, and recovered self.

Let us help you recover. It is your time to be healed. Let no one shame you into believing that you shouldn't have limitations. Let no one convince you that you shouldn't have needs.

Pause Before You Break, Way Before You Break

We all have breaking points. Yet, you are best served if you do not push yourself to your breaking point. Let no other person drive you to your breaking point, either. Their style is not what is necessarily your style. Their truth is not yours. Their limits are not yours. Their energy is not yours. Their past, their body, their support system, their immune system, their coping style, their future, their outside world…is not yours. What you experience is not theirs either.

You are uniquely you.
You have strengths others do not have.
You have weaknesses others do not understand.
You have stress-triggers only you possess.

As a consequence, you must manage your exposure to trauma and how you are reacting based upon who you are and not upon what someone else believes you should be. Heal your trauma reactions based on your style, not based on someone else's style.

When you have provided health care, caregiving, or medical interventions in *situations that are traumatic for you*, respect that what impacts you is not always what will impact someone else in the same way.

If you have experienced trauma in your past, as a child or teen or young adult, likely you will react uniquely when facing distressing situations as a caregiver. If you have never experienced trauma before, facing medical sufferings will impact you differently too.

Do not compare your personal reactions to traumatic medical situations with any other person's reaction *unless it helps you cope better, and it helps you find compassion for yourself.*

Design Your Personal Paths to Recovery

Furthermore, you must design your recovery program. Your path to recovery from exposure to traumatic medical situations will be YOUR PATH. You will recover from any Secondary Traumatic Stress disorder in your unique way because you are uniquely you.

This book offers hundreds of tools that help people recover from exposure to traumas. Please experiment with the different interventions provided. Find your unique recipe for recovery that works for you today. Later, perhaps other tools become more useful for tomorrow or next month.

I have worked in the trauma recovery world for over 40 years with deployed soldiers, abused children, raped adults, tortured spouses, fire devastations, flood or earthquake disasters, severely ill patients, maimed accident victims, and much more.

Every person recovers from trauma in their personal fashion using their own collection of tools of interventions, social support, and decisions.

You and I will explore different recovery tools which you can try-out to see which collection of tools best suits the following:

- your history
- your temperament
- your personality
- your coping styles
- your support system
- your neurology
- your physical, emotional and mental styles
- your most recent exposure to trauma work
- your previous exposure to trauma
- the intensity of trauma you faced or are facing

While breezing through the chapters that follow, you will check off *your honest issues* and *those tools which match* your situation and your personality. Let's work together to tailor a program which helps you recover your physical well-being, your emotional joy, your sense of ease, and your professional satisfaction. Write notes in the margins, highlight, check off lists, argue your ideas, reject what does not fit now, and try what seems workable for now.

Here are three helpful suggestions from this first chapter. *Check off those which suit you today* and mark those you might want to try next week or next month.

Checklist of Tools Offered in Chapter 1 and Introduction

_____ 1. Check the 12R's mentioned in the Introduction and write notes next to those which concern me.

_____ 2. Consider contacting Dr. Carol Francis at TherapyCounselingCoaching.com.

_____ 3. Consider joining the online group on Facebook, offered by Dr. Carol Francis to create the social support I wish as part of my recovery tools. Go to: Abuse and Trauma Recovery Group – which I run at this link: https://www.facebook.com/groups/2108549269424755

_____ 4. Consider signing up for the Courses on Trauma Recovery for Health Care Trauma Workers the Abuse and Trauma Recovery website, https://abusetraumarecovery.com/HealthCareWorkersTraumaRecovery. (At this site, you can take each of the 112 classes laid out in 13 courses for Survivors and 6 Courses specifically designed for Health Care Givers' Trauma Recovery. Please visit the blog on AbuseTraumaRecovery.com as well for daily updated tools.)

The aim is to help you in a manner like you help hundreds.

Let me thank you.

Let me help you in return, now.

Together, let's tame the tiger of trauma in your life.

Empowerment by Carol A. Francis

Those Who Have Known Suffering

"The most beautiful people
we have known are
those who have known defeat,
known suffering,
known struggle,
known loss,
and have found their way out of the depths.

These persons
have an appreciation,
a sensitivity,
and an understanding of life
that fills them with compassion,
gentleness, and a deep loving concern.
Beautiful people do not just happen."

Dr. Elisabeth Kübler-Ross

Chapter 2
Trauma's Impact on YOU

Time for Self-Honesty and Reflection

Your recipe for recovery will depend on the impact your traumatic situations hurled upon you. If you feel confused about your reactions of depression, anxiety, anger, sadness, stress, burnout, fatigue, nightmares, sleeplessness, depersonalization, numbness, and so forth, *this chapter will help you appreciate your personal reactions to your unique exposure to trauma.*

First, privately, answer the following questionnaires. You will look inside yourself and discover how your **Secondary Post Traumatic Stress** is expressing itself. Or you will face how your **Compassion Fatigue** is showing-up and robbing you of your Compassion Satisfaction. Or you will consider if you are professionally and personally **Burned-Out**.

As Healthcare Workers, we often push ourselves too far because there is ALWAYS someone needing our help. We sacrifice our body's health, our personality's liveliness, connections with family and friends, and our recuperation time because we know people need our help.

"NEED" will never disappear. Thank you for trying to help as much as possible. But you sacrificing your life is not advisable for your well-being and not beneficial to many people who love you and want to enjoy you, including yourself.

As a Healthcare Workers, you likely recognize in your patients the symptoms of PTSD. Yet, it is always harder to recognize PTSD or SPTS in ourselves. We grow accustom to functioning under stressful circumstances that are high demand and potentially life-threatening. You have GRIT and RESILIENCE, and that makes you good at your job, vital to your workforce.

Everyone, though, has their tipping-point, their breaking-point. Yet, it may be harder for you to see yourself than to see others. Can you experience that you have reached your limit? Can you come to terms with your need to admit that you have been traumatized and need to repair, renew, and recover?

These questionnaires are the first steps so you can discover if you are suffering from some type or some degree of trauma. Now let's do these questionnaires first. Discover how much trauma your body, brain, emotions, personality, and spirit all need to heal.

Secondary Post-Traumatic Stress Reactions

First step, rate any of the following reactions to trauma you currently endure. Be honest with yourself. Be clear about your reactions. Be compassionate with your needs.

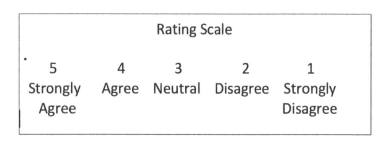

Rating Scale

5	4	3	2	1
Strongly Agree	Agree	Neutral	Disagree	Strongly Disagree

_____ 1. I have reoccurring, unwanted, or distressing memories of traumatic events.

_____ 2. I relive the traumatic events as if they were happening again.

_____ 3. I have upsetting dreams or nightmares about the traumatic events.

_____ 4. I have severe emotional distress or physical reactions to some things that remind me of the traumatic events.

_____ 5. I try to avoid thinking or talking about the traumatic events.

_____ 6. I avoid places, activities, or people that remind me of the traumatic events.

_____ 7. I have negative thoughts about myself, other people, or the world.

_____ 8. I feel hopeless about my future.

_____ 9. I seem to have memory problems, including not remembering important aspects of the traumatic events.

_____ 10. I currently have difficulty maintaining close relationships.

_____ 11. I feel detached from family and friends.

_____ 12. I currently lack interest in activities I once enjoyed.

_____ 13. I have difficulty experiencing positive emotions.

_____ 14. I feel emotionally numb.

_____ 15. I have been easily startled or frightened.

_____ 16. I've been on-guard for danger.

_____ 17. I am indulging in self-destructive behavior, such as drinking too much, drug use, or driving too fast.

_____ 18. I'm having trouble sleeping.

_____ 19. I'm having trouble concentrating.

_____ 20. I am irritable, having angry outbursts, or aggressive behaviors.

_____ 21. I am having overwhelming guilt or shame.

_____ 22. Sometimes I feel like I am re-enacting the traumatic event or aspects of the traumatic event through play, conversation, thoughts, memories, or relationships.

To score, tally your answers below.

_____ Strongly Agree (5)
_____ Agree (4)
_____ Neutral (3)
_____ Disagree (2)
_____ Strongly Disagree (1)

To gain a sense of the severity you are facing, total your score of "Strongly Agree" and "Agree" and compare your total with your tally of "Disagree" and "Strongly Disagree." These scores will help you evaluate how much more you are suffering in contrast with how much you are not suffering from traumatically induced PTSD, or Secondary Post-Traumatic Stress (SPTS or STS).

Compassion Fatigue and Professional Burn-Out

The above questions address SPTP, Secondary Post-Traumatic Stress or STS, Secondary Traumatic Stress. The above set of questions helps you recognize the degree to which you are actually reacting to your exposure to your patients' ordeals while helping. Now, let's find out if you are dealing with what some researchers call *Compassion Fatigue.*

Compassion Fatigue and ProQOL Questionnaire

Compassion Fatigue is a condition named by Dr. Beth Hudnall Stamm. She developed questionnaires that help you evaluate your level of professional satisfaction while working with those in need.

Please take this free questionnaire next. By permission, it is copied here on the next three pages for you. The Center for Victims of Torture, further detailed at www.ProQOL.org, has given all professionals the right to copy and use their worthy materials for free because they care. How absolutely wonderful! I have copied their materials for your convenience so you can go through this questionnaire without delay.

COMPASSION SATISFACTION AND COMPASSION FATIGUE
(PROQOL) VERSION 5 (2009)

When you [help] people you have direct contact with their lives. As you may have found, your compassion for those you [help] can affect you in positive and negative ways. Below are some questions about your experiences, both positive and negative, as a [helper]. Consider each of the following questions about you and your current work situation. Select the number that honestly reflects how frequently you experienced these things in the last 30 days.

1=Never	2=Rarely	3=Sometimes	4=Often	5=Very Often

____ 1. I am happy.

____ 2. I am preoccupied with more than one person I [help].

____ 3. I get satisfaction from being able to [help] people.

____ 4. I feel connected to others.

____ 5. I jump or am startled by unexpected sounds.

____ 6. I feel invigorated after working with those I [help].

____ 7. I find it difficult to separate my personal life from my life as a [helper].

____ 8. I am as not as productive at work because I am losing sleep over traumatic experiences of a person I [help].

____ 9. I think that I might have been affected by the traumatic stress of those I [help].

____ 10. I feel trapped by my job as a [helper].

____ 11. Because of my [helping], I have felt "on edge" about various things.

____ 12. I like my work as a [helper].

____ 13. I feel depressed because of the traumatic experiences of the people I [help].

____ 14. I feel as though I am experiencing the trauma of someone I have [helped].

____ 15. I have beliefs that sustain me.

____ 16. I am pleased with how I am able to keep up with [helping] techniques and protocols.

____ 17. I am the person I always wanted to be.

____ 18. My work makes me feel satisfied.

____ 19. I feel worn out because of my work as a [helper].

____ 20. I have happy thoughts and feelings about those I [help] and how I could help them.

____ 21. I feel overwhelmed because my case [work] load seems endless.

____ 22. I believe I can make a difference through my work.

____ 23. I avoid certain activities or situations because they remind me of frightening experiences of the people I [help].

____ 24. I am proud of what I can do to [help].

____ 25. As a result of my [helping], I have intrusive, frightening thoughts.

____ 26. I feel "bogged down" by the system.

____ 27. I have thoughts that I am a "success" as a [helper].

____ 28. I can't recall important parts of my work with trauma victims.

____ 29. I am a very caring person.

____ 30. I am happy that I chose to do this work.

Based on your responses, place your personal scores below. If you have any concerns, you should discuss them with a physical or mental health care professional.

Compassion Satisfaction _____

Compassion satisfaction is about the pleasure you derive from being able to do your work well. For example, you may feel like it is a pleasure to help others through your work. You may feel positively about your colleagues or your ability to contribute to the work setting or even the greater good of society. Higher scores on this scale represent a greater satisfaction related to your ability to be an effective caregiver in your job.

If you are in the higher range, you probably derive a good deal of professional satisfaction from your position. If your scores are below 23, you may either find problems with your job, or there may be some other reason—for example, you might derive your satisfaction from activities other than your job. (Alpha scale reliability 0.88)

Burnout_____

Most people have an intuitive idea of what burnout is. From the research perspective, burnout is one of the elements of Compassion Fatigue (CF). It is associated with feelings of hopelessness and difficulties in dealing with work or in doing your job effectively. These negative feelings usually have a gradual onset. They can reflect the feeling that your efforts make no difference, or they can be associated with a very high workload or a non-supportive work environment. Higher scores on this scale mean that you are at higher risk for burnout.

If your score is below 23, this probably reflects positive feelings about your ability to be effective in your work. If you score above 41, you may wish to think about what at work makes you feel like you are not effective in your position. Your score may reflect your mood; perhaps you were having a "bad day" or are in need of some time off. If the high score persists or if it is reflective of other worries, it may be a cause for concern. (Alpha scale reliability 0.75)

Secondary Traumatic Stress_____

The second component of Compassion Fatigue (CF) is secondary traumatic stress (STS). It is about your work related, secondary exposure to extremely or traumatically stressful events. Developing problems due to exposure to other's trauma is somewhat rare but does happen to many people who care for those who have experienced extremely or traumatically stressful events. For example, you may repeatedly hear stories about the traumatic things that happen to other people, commonly called Vicarious Traumatization. If your work puts you directly in the path of danger, for example, field work in a war or area of civil violence, this is not secondary exposure; your exposure is primary. However, if you are exposed to others' traumatic events as a result of your work, for example, as a therapist or an emergency worker, this is secondary exposure. The symptoms of STS are usually rapid in onset and associated with a particular event. They may include being afraid, having difficulty sleeping, having images of the upsetting event pop into your mind, or avoiding things that remind you of the event.

If your score is above 41, you may want to take some time to think about what at work may be frightening to you or if there is some other reason for the elevated score. While higher scores do not mean that you do have a problem, they are an indication that you may want to examine how you feel about your work and your work environment. You may wish to discuss this with your supervisor, a colleague, or a health care professional. (Alpha scale reliability 0.81)

In this section, you will score your test so you understand the interpretation for you. To find your score on **each section,** total the questions listed on the left and then find your score in the table on the right of the section.

Compassion Satisfaction Scale

Copy your rating on each of these questions on to this table and add them up. When you have added then up you can find your score on the table to the right.

3. ____
6. ____
12. ____
16. ____
18. ____
20. ____
22. ____
24. ____
27. ____
30. ____

Total: ____

The sum of my Compassion Satisfaction questions is	And my Compassion Satisfaction level is
22 or less	Low
Between 23 and 41	Moderate
42 or more	High

Burnout Scale

On the burnout scale you will need to take an extra step. Starred items are "reverse scored." If you scored the item 1, write a 5 beside it. The reason we ask you to reverse the scores is because scientifically the measure works better when these questions are asked in a positive way though they can tell us more about their negative form. For example, question 1. "I am happy" tells us more about

You Wrote	Change to
	5
2	4
3	3
4	2
5	1

the effects of helping when you are not happy so you reverse the score

*1. ____ = ____
*4. ____ = ____
8. ____
10. ____
*15. ____ = ____
*17. ____ = ____
19. ____
21. ____
26. ____
*29. ____ = ____

Total: ____

The sum of my Burnout Questions is	And my Burnout level is
22 or less	Low
Between 23 and 41	Moderate
42 or more	High

Secondary Traumatic Stress Scale

Just like you did on Compassion Satisfaction, copy your rating on each of these questions on to this table and add them up. When you have added them up you can find your score on the table to the right.

2. ____
5. ____
7. ____
9. ____
11. ____
13. ____
14. ____
23. ____
25. ____
28. ____

Total: ____

The sum of my Secondary Trauma questions is	And my Secondary Traumatic Stress level is
22 or less	Low
Between 23 and 41	Moderate
42 or more	High

21

Summarize Your Professional Quality of Life Survey

What did you discover about yourself from this Professional Quality of Life Survey? Write down your insights by answering these questions, privately.

1. Can I admit that I am having strong reactions to what I have experienced? If so, how do I describe myself in this state?

2. Do I feel that it is impacting my relationships more than I realized? If so, how so?

3. Do I notice that my work has impacted my emotional and mental well-being more than I want to admit? If so, how so?

4. Do I feel ashamed, embarrassed, overly dramatic, when I admit that I am having very strong reactions? If so, describe what you notice.

5. Do I worry that others may judge me, ridicule me, pressure me, or misunderstand any of my Secondary Traumatic Stress reactions or my Compassion Fatigue? If so, who? How do I deal with them?

Stamm and her research team and affiliated research findings explained Compassion Fatigue this way:

> We have learned that neither Vicarious Traumatization or Compassion Fatigue are synonyms of PTDS or of secondary traumatic stress (Figley & Roop, 2006; Pearlman & Carnigi, 2009; Stamm, 2006; Stamm, 2010). People can experience negative effects of secondary exposure without developing a psychological disorder such as PTSD. Compassion Fatigue is not a diagnosis. It is possible that Compassion Fatigue is a descriptive term and that a person struggling with Compassion Fatigue also has a psychological disorder. For example, people who suffer with burnout may also have a diagnosable level of depression. Similarly, people may have a diagnosable level of PTSD or some other mental, emotional or physical disorder that is likely linked to their experience of compassion fatigue. Increasing importance is being placed on resiliency and transformation of negative to positive aspects (Pearlman & Carnigi, 2009; Stamm & Figley, 2009; Stamm, Figley & Figley, 2010).

Here is a diagram, Stamm and The Center for Victims of Torture, provide for your further understanding at www.ProQOL.org.

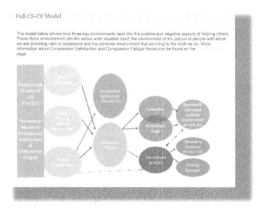

Understanding and Respecting Yourself

Since everyone is different, the negative and positive impact of trauma work is not the same for each individual. No two people suffer, survive or recover the same way.

Please respect your way of suffering,
your way of enduring,
your way of surviving, and
your way of recovering.

Some are supercharged by intensity and severity of medical emergencies. Some absorb tremendous mojo when helping during extremely horrible circumstances because of their strong sense of purpose or their fundamental optimism and curiosity. Some enjoy extreme sports and in like manner some enjoy the rush of urgent situations.

Others robotically obey or comply with demands. People can also feel the reward of being a "true soldier" for a cause. Some are emotionally detached from most of life and do not empathically feel the impact of complications, yet they may manifest symptoms physically or socially. Some enjoy the teamwork of tackling huge tasks together and reap the positive aspects of the social team regardless of the job.

Some are driven by compassion, love, or empathy and as long as those emotional resources are strong, they feel positive about their trauma-work intervention efforts.

Some are driven by ego, self-esteem, or superiority and use trauma-work to prove their importance. Some believe that duty and strength of character are above all other needs, charging forth regardless of frustrations or severity of situations.

Everyone is different. Who are you? What combination of qualities do you possess which help you avoid SPTS or Compassion Fatigue (CF) or Burnout? Do you survive trauma work better than those individuals who have no wish nor any capacity to help during extreme crises or traumatic situations?

Why Did You Choose Trauma Work?

Answer these questions here:

1) Why are you involved in trauma work?

2) What pleasures or satisfactions do you gain from trauma work?

3) What qualities of your past, your personality, and your training make you uniquely qualified for trauma work?

Qualities that Mismatch People with Trauma Work

Conversely, which combination of qualities do you honorably possess which can lead you into a Secondary Post Traumatic Stress reaction, or Compassion Fatigue or Professional Burnout? Rate the items below which pertain to you.

Rating Scale				
5	4	3	2	1
Strongly Agree	Agree	Neutral	Disagree	Strongly Disagree

_____ 1. I am quite sensitive to the pains of others.

_____ 2. I cannot separate other's pain from my pain at times since I am empathic.

_____ 3. I bring my work home with me often.

_____ 4. I can't separate work from playtime.

_____ 5. I secretly dislike my co-workers or my superiors.

_____ 6. I dread waking up on workdays.

_____ 7. I absorb the hopelessness of situations quickly.

_____ 8. I blame myself for any failures.

_____ 9. I wish I could work by myself more.

_____10. I refuel myself better when I am alone.

_____ 11. When situations and people are negative, sad, or hopeless around me, I become very dark and morbid too.

_____ 12. I can't stand being around needy, desperate people.

These questions help you reflect on the reasons why trauma work may not be your forte currently. These 12 questions are limited, you are not. Write down why you believe you may not be suitable for trauma work as an on-going professional pursuit. Then write down why you believe you are suitable for trauma work. Compare.

Why I am not suitable for Trauma work (anymore or never):

Signs of Professional Burnout (Bit Different from SPTS & CF)

When you can no longer feel compassion, empathy, joy, happiness, sadness, grief, hope, pleasure, success, or moments of worry, then you likely have *emotionally burned out.*

When you mentally want to forget work-related tasks, wish to ignore co-workers or patients, resent time spent at work, return home grumpy and antagonistic, think of work as only a paycheck then you likely have *mental burnout.*

If you often feel fatigued, move slower, or drag before having to go to work or if you develop physical symptoms such as headaches or body aches, you likely have physical burnout that is psychologically stimulated by *being professionally burned out.*

Chronic or "too much" trauma exposure also aggravates burnouts. Perhaps, you need to find another line of work, another employment, or different arrangement to refresh your vigor or passions. Maybe, this current work situation is bleeding you of your liveliness.

We become numb sometimes as a means of coping with being overloaded, overextended, or physically exhausted. Being numb helps us extend our work, our efforts, or our schedule beyond normal limits. Please be honest with yourself and admit if you are overextending yourself beyond your natural resources and beyond your personal style.

Past Traumas Impact Our Current Traumatic Reactions

Now, it will also be necessary for you to appreciate the impact of past traumas (or abuses) you experienced as a child or teenager. Your past will also potentially factor into how you might adversely react to traumatic events in your adult years.

Sometimes, past traumas, which were *successfully managed*, build resilience, determination, passionate commitment, and tenacity. Past traumas for some build stamina and muscles to help others with their traumas. Sometimes, past traumas create sensitivities or trigger points which make trauma work undesirable.

The CDC-Kaiser Permanente Adverse Childhood Experiences (ACE) is one of the largest studies conducted which helps us understand how our past traumas impact our future coping styles and sensitivities. Go now to this link to take the ACE test:

https://www.npr.org/sections/health-shots/2015/03/02/387007941/take-the-ace-quiz-and-learn-what-it-does-and-doesnt-mean

This ACE test is a simple and private questionnaire that helps you discern the impact your past traumas or abuses might have upon your current sensitivities to trauma exposure as an adult. Have respect for your vulnerabilities. Conduct your life and decisions in ways most suitable for your personality qualities and your honest needs in life. The higher your score, the more vulnerable you are to future complications unless you have recovered significantly from the effects.

To help you recover from past traumas and abuses, please read my book ***Paths to Recovery After Abuse and Trauma*** and take any or all of the Courses prepared for you at *AbuseTraumaRecovery.com* for a very inexpensive donation.

Moving from Trauma Work to Recovery

We took this chapter to help you recognize your authentic trauma reactions. These different tools enable you to consider what you have endured. Such may adversely impact your mind, emotions, physicality, and spirituality.

Now that you have examined and faced these personal truths about yourself, it is time to develop a recipe toward your recovery, your renewal.

Having worked for four decades in the Trauma-Recovery field with thousands of people, I now conclude that no one recipe fits all people. No one path takes every person to the same destination of recovery. As we move through the next chapters, which are all recovery-oriented, please pick and choose those practices, ideas, and suggestions which match your needs and style today. You can use other tools that match your needs tomorrow or next week.

Whatever tools you choose, let's both keep our eyes on the goal of your recovery. We want you to renew yourself, re-invigorate yourself, heal yourself, and create the new version of yourself that is filled with passion, creativity, satisfaction, and energy.

Checklist of Tools Offered in Chapter 2

Check off those tools below from Chapter 2 you wish to implement today.

_____ 1. STS checklist of post-trauma reactions, taken, scored and evaluated.

_____ 2. Professional Quality of Life checklist, taken, scored, and reflected upon pertaining to Sympathy Fatigue and Professional Burn-out.

_____ 3. Checklist for Sensitivities to Burn-out, Trauma Fatigue or Compassion Fatigue.

_____ 4. ACE questionnaire regarding the impact of past childhood trauma or abuse.

_____ 5. Suitability for Trauma Work Personal Reflection written.

_____ 6. Read ***Paths to Recovery After Abuse and Trauma*** by Dr. Carol Francis.

_____ 7. Use any or all of the Courses offered on *AbuseTraumaRecovery.com* offered for survivors of past traumas and abuse.

_____ 8. Use of any or all of the Courses offered for Health Care Workers' Trauma Recovery at AbuseTraumaRecovery.com/HealthCareWorkersTraumaRecovery.

BEATHE Deeply for ONE MINUTE

DRINK WATER,

Cool and Clean All Day

SLEEP with Dedication

EAT with Celebration

MOVE with Enjoyment

These basics, for biological creatures,

are nonnegotiable for

Inner Peace to be renewed.

Own Your Peace: KISS Method for Inner Peaceful Living

by Dr. Carol Francis

Chapter 3
Recalibrate Your Physical Self-Care

Physical self-care is typically the first to disappear during trauma-work. Sleep is sacrificed. Quality food is skipped and replaced with simple carbs, stress eating. Regular water hydration is substituted with dehydrating "energy" drinks. Exercise is relegated to the "luxury" category. Inner peace is replaced with helpless, anxious, and depressed feelings.

When exposed to trauma, people can lose all regulation, rhythms, and consistent patterns that help each part of your body function reliably and smoothly. Chapter 3 focuses on how you can assist your body's recovery so that you can rely on your body as you emotionally and psychologically recover simultaneously.

You want to shift your body's dysregulations after your trauma exposure so it can function smoothly. You need to create reliable rhythms or patterns so that your body can regulate itself and support you reliably. Take charge and exercise the power you have to help your body recover – TODAY!

We must reverse habits and patterns we adapted during our trauma work. Returning to and embracing healthy patterns celebrates our body's essential strengths.

Foods that Renews Your Body

Begin today. Right now.

> ➢ Grab 10 ounces of water and drink it generously.
> ➢ Next, eat vegetables and fruits, fresh and crunchy when possible. Aim for 5-10 per day.
> ➢ Select protein, fresh and free of inessential fats to eat three times today.
> ➢ Grains also are important for de-stressing as they are rich in B-Vitamins and fibers, as well.

You knew all of these worthy eating habits. Yes? Now practice them with very little debate even if you don't want to. Be mechanical about returning to eating right as a gift to your body's desperate need to restart it and to return to functioning smoothly.

Your mouth and desires probably will not match your urge to eat healthy food until you reset your body's cravings away from stress-eating foods that are not nutritious. If you can't slow down eating refined sugars, saturated fats, caffeine, or simple carbs today, then at least EAT these healthy foods until your body becomes more accustomed to GOOD foods than to junk foods for fuel.

For more help on switching into healthy eating, please feel free to read my book: *If You Can't Stop Eating, Maybe You're Hungry: Reset Your Cravings* easily attainable as an eBook via Amazon or Kindle.

Sleep that Refreshes and Heals

Sleep is next in importance. Avoid those foods and drinks that interfere with your body's sleep cycles first. Caffeine, sugar, lack of water, and hard-to-digest foods hours before sleep will impede your body's and brain's rest cycle.

Establish a Sleeping Ritual

Go to bed initially at the same time for at least 2 weeks. Create a pre-bedtime ritual that signals your body and brain to shut down peacefully. Such rituals include reading distracting boring books, sex, massage, prayer, yoga, singing, music, audiobooks, or podcast. Some can watch a television show that calms and distracts them, but be careful about screen time that keeps your brain wrestling actively so that it cannot shut down.

Some people sleep best with silence, others with music. Some sleep with low-light and others in darkness. Typically, sleeping at nighttime refreshes the body better than sleeping during the daylight hours. Do your best to optimize your sleep.

Take progressive steps to retrain your body and brain to sleep. Studies are clear that our bodies adapt to stress, to poor eating habits, and to poor sleeping patterns in order to survive. Conversely, we actually have to RETRAIN our body to adapt to healthy eating and good deep sleep patterns when the urgent and traumatic events have passed.

You must retrain your body and mind to adapt to healthy foods.
You may need to retrain yourself to sleep soundly again.
Make progress one step at a time, one meal at a time, or one sleep cycle at a time.

Movement that Balances, Strengthens, Refreshes

Move hourly to stretch sore and stiff muscles and bones. Move hourly to rebalance your left with your right and your front with your back. Move to strengthen your muscles. Move hourly to create sweat and blood circulation. Move hourly to ignite deep breathing that cleanses your lungs. Move creatively to connect your brain functions to your limbs. Move to de-stress and renew.

As with eating and sleeping, you will need to RETRAIN your body day by day to be more flexible, balanced, and strong.

Be patient with your daily progress.
Yet take progressive steps every day!

Yoga and Isometrics Just for You

For your benefit, Yoga and Isometric Exercises are provided for free at:

AbuseTraumaRecovery.com/HealthCareWorkersTrauma Recovery, Course 3 by a wonderfully sensitive Yoga teacher, Adrienne, who offered these courses to be added to this site to help you recover your body, mind and spirit through movement. Please enjoy. Please move.

Eat, Sleep, Move

These three practices are so simple to reinstitute into your life. However, initially, you will need to be structured and disciplined because you will likely be unmotivated to apply effort to your new body's practices.

Under stress and trauma, we adapt horrible habits and our body submits and supports us the best ways it can. Our body's ability to adapt is incredible. Of course, eventually, our body will breakdown, and we have to build it up again, day by day.

If you need a metaphor, imagine this: Envision a garden destroyed by draught and fungus. For a bit, it survives but eventually it collapses. It takes effort, dedication, and reliability to cultivate the garden's healthy ability to produce vegetables and flowers. Your body's entire system needs to be regrown. The formula for success is easy:

Eat well.

Sleep well.

Move well.

As mentioned before, if you need daily motivation and more information, you can access online courses at:

AbuseTraumaRecovery.com/HealthCareWorkersTraumaRecovery

Your body's recovery is the second course with 6 videos, 12 motivational exercises, and 12 quick meditations that help you renew your body's health. Please receive that support from me for your entire team.

Checklist of Tools Offered in Chapter 3

Check off those tools below from Chapter 3 you wish to implement today.

_____ 1. Eat 5-10 Veggies Today

_____ 2. Drink 64 ounces of refreshing WATER today.

_____ 3. Eat health protein 3-5 times TODAY.

_____ 4. Reduce junk food today.

_____ 5. Reduce foods that interfere with sleeping today.

_____ 6. Go to bed at the same time for two weeks, starting today.

_____ 7. Establish a workable bedtime ritual that makes me sleepy, starting today.

_____ 8. Begin to train my brain and body to sleep better and better each day, starting today.

_____ 9. Today, I will stretch, balance and strengthen my muscles and heart several times and work my way up to a regular exercise routine and an hourly movement practice.

_____ 10. I can read *If You Can't Stop Eating, Maybe You're Hungry: Reset Your Cravings* today if I need some encouragement and clarity about my renewed eating patterns.

_____ 11. I can review Courses on AbuseTraumaRecovery.com, which address my body's well-being and recovery.

_____ 12. I can review Courses on AbuseTraumaRecovery.com/HealthCareWorkersTraumaRecovery program that pertain to my body's recovery from trauma.

Chapter 4
Rebuilding Inner Peace

Horrors. Chaos. Hopelessness.
Unavoidable devastations.
Unnecessary travesties. Inevitable losses.

You faced each of these to different intensities, quantities, and levels of personal involvement as both witness and participant. As a Health Care Worker, you were helpful beyond measure even with impossible odds.

You effortfully pushed yourself beyond comfort and ease. People owe their lives to you and your team. Very hard work. Struggles occurred too complicated to describe adequately. As a consequence,

You likely lost your sense of inner peacefulness.

Rebuild Your Skills to Create Inner Peace

Now, as part of your recovery, it is time to rebuild your interior landscape where peacefulness can flourish in your own life even though you know others who may never have a chance for peacefulness again.

When humans are exposed to ongoing trauma, every physical, emotional, and mental system is disrupted in order to adapt to intense pacing, efforts, and complications. As a consequence, every part of who you are has to recalibrate in order to once again 1) experience peacefulness when peaceful moments occur, and 2) create peacefulness internally whenever possible with relative ease.

In my book *__Own Your Peace: KISS Method for Inner Peaceful Living__*, hundreds of tools are provided that help individuals receive, experience, create, and share many levels of Inner Peace. I refer you there if you wish to dive deeper.

Also, as a resource just for you, my online courses for *HealthCareWorkersTraumaRecovery,* which is on **AbuseTraumaRecovery.com,** has 6 short classes designed to help you understand and experience inner peace after being traumatized. You will find 12 beautifully relaxing and meaningful meditations prepared for you that are quick and easy to use over and over again as you retrain your internal emotional and mental world to experience peacefulness.

Of course, the following pages will also guide you so you can wake-up your inner peacefulness. Let's get started.

Three Depths of Inner Peace

Quickly, I want you to recognize there are three depths of inner peace. In this chapter, we stimulate the first two depths of your inner peaceful domain. The three depths are:

 ➢ Serendipitous Blissful Moments
 ➢ Self-Created Inner Peace
 ➢ Ascendant and Transcendent Inner Peace

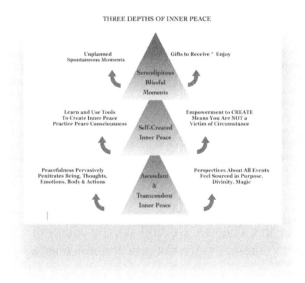

THREE DEPTHS OF INNER PEACE

Serendipitous Blissful Moments

Blissful Moments serendipitously wash briefly into your life. These whispers of spontaneous peace happen without any effort nor anticipation. They quickly shower upon you.

Sudden sincere laughter of your toddler
Unexpected flowers from a neighbor's garden
Wisps of butterflies floating overhead
Thank you cards from patients' families
Smile from a colleague
Kind unexpected gift
Fragrance of scented candles or BBQ
Unexpected moneys to help pay the past due bills

Something inside you resonates with these moments briefly as you pause to sigh deeply. You might gratefully soak in these moments of peacefulness.

However, because your mind and emotions have adapted to coping with painful traumatic moments, you can easily miss out on these spontaneous Serendipitous Blissful Moments. You might be blinded by your focus on urgency, emergencies, stress, anxiety, or depression instead. In this chapter, we will retrain your mind and emotions to tune-in to pleasant peacefulness once again.

When you receive these peaceful moments as gifts, you allow yourself to be present in that experience of your inner peace. Allowing these sudden moments inside you, is the first depth of inner peace. Here is a playful metaphor.

Parable of Hungry Rats

Alley rats ragefully rambled through a small kitchen trash can, scurrying through moldy breads and dank cheeses. They were blinded by their starvation. They are unaware that the restaurant's refrigerator door - inches away – is open accidentally. The refrigerator is filled with gourmet breads, meats, and fruits that would supply hundreds of starving rats to gourmet treats.

Exercises below and on AbuseTraumaRecovery.com will enable you once again tune-in to peaceful experiences when these Serendipitous Blissful Moments occur right in front of you. On that site, you will hear audios that include guided imagery, meditations, mindfulness practices and instruction that will wake-up your mind and emotions to sense these unpredictable pleasant moments.

Self-Created Inner Peace

Being able deliberately to *create inner* peaceful moments, despite all the negatives you have experienced or the torment that troubles your mind, is the second depth of Inner Peace. At this level, you create and dwell upon what peaceful activities *you design and* what *you direct* toward your own mind, emotions, spirit or body.

Deciding to create Inner Peace is this second depth. Learning how to create Inner Peace is one of your powers. You deliberately engage your thoughts, feelings, body and soul in exercises and activities that move you toward Inner Peace. You shift consciously. You constructively design your moments, your plans, your decisions, your interactions, and other aspects of your life to cultivate Inner Peace.

Sara writes poems.
Ted jogs on park trails.
Randy and his wife climb rocks.
Jack lies on his bed, listening to Alternative Music with earphones.
Tandy sings while playing guitar.
Jenny channels Angels or Spirit Guides.
Rob composes music.
Carol paints and draws.
Henry plays racket ball.
Karen bakes cakes.
Jim prays.
Cathy watches classic musicals.
Alexa games online.
Hugh programs software.

Thousands of activities can be implemented that shift you into planned periods of Inner Peace. These planned moments are escapes that help you forget, distract, refresh, renew and recalibrate.

Let me create these moments for you quickly. I call these Zen Zone Meditations. I also provide some Zen Zone Meditations for you on AbuseTraumaRecovery.com. In this chapter, however, merely follow these quick instructions to the best of your ability and flexibility. Here we go:

ZEN ZONE MEDITATION MOMENT
Quickly flow from one expression listed below to the next. Faking it or acting it out is fine. Shift rapidly. Have fun.

Cry

Smile

Laugh

Frown then Laugh

Yoga's Lion's Face

Shout and Yell then Laugh

Watch or imagine a sunset or sunrise or moonrise

Imagine or stare at stars (and satellites)

Imagine or listen to crickets

Imagine walking in nature

Mentally imagine one memory of a peaceful moment

Mentally imagine sitting with people who are peaceful

Mentally remember a meaningful, gentle, sensual kiss

Online now, read poetry or inspirational writing

Finish by listening to gentle or pleasant music for a moment.

If you do each of these for five seconds using your imagination, you are actually retraining yourself to create inner peace. Doing any collection pleasant memories or thoughts teaches your brain, body and emotions to resonate with peaceful moments. As you deliberately decide to activate such thoughts and memories, you will also be deliberately training yourself to CREATE inner peace. You also will begin to empathetically harmonize with the experience of peacefulness happening around you.

Doing this sequence of instructions will increase your ability to slip into experiences of inner peacefulness upon your command. You will learn to create peaceful experiences inside you and then practice participating in those experiences.

Practicing this exercise for 60 seconds a few times a day will retrain your mind, emotions, body and spirit to dive into peacefulness instead of traumatic memories. In addition, when traumatic feelings of anxiety or panic intrude upon you or when traumatic memories or worries engulf your mind, you will be able consciously to shift your focus because you have practiced creating peaceful moments. As you actively participate mentally and emotionally in the quiet moments you become a creator of those moments.

Some researchers call these exercises mindfulness practice. Others designated this long ago as meditation. Yoga instructors might call this your Shavasana. Other practitioners might call this self-hypnosis, trance work, quantum consciousness, Theta consciousness, delta brain wave.

I call this my **Zen Zone**s, and an endless number of imaginings, memories, or activities can create a zen-like zone in which you can dwell. Zen Zone moments can be summoned by you when your mind is kidnapped by horrific memories or your awful emotions. As you retrain yourself, you can create a Zen Zone inside you that wards of stampeding panic, grief, guilt, shame or sorrow.

You must, however, practice creating and entering into these Zen Zones so that when situations become tough, you have mastered these skills. Creating inner peace is a learned skill, especially when you have been exposed to turmoil chronically.

Forty More Suggestions of 2 Minute Zen-Zone Moments

A Meditation on Humane Grief

This afternoon, I cried out loud for those poisoned by Michigan government's toxic water policy. I forced a yogic angry Lion's Face to express my anger. I shouted, yelled, and then sighed for a minute. I returned to loudly crying and shouting in between. Then I raised my hands over my head, straightened my posture and prayed for wisdom to act helpfully. I wrote a proactive bit and posted to my social network to voice my intent to care proactively. How to be politically and socially helpful pragmatically is a question that will steer my actions for months to come. I also wrote another note to a friend who lost his mom this week. These 15 minutes relieved so much tension, and compassion flourished.

Inner Peace Conversations

1. Quietly talk with pets, plants, or inanimate objects, out loud or in your thoughts.

2. Prepare quick questions about peace for future conversations with strangers, family members (etc.) that may generate moments of laughter, kindness, peacefulness, joy. Weave these questions into conversations. You will be surprised how responsive and thoughtful people become. Their peacefulness will exude as well. Peacefulness is contagious. Your powerfulness in generating peacefulness for yourself and others will grow.

3. Quickly write Self-Expressions about Peacefulness (Journal, Haiku, Letters, Social Networking).

4. Physically connect with peaceful expressions by dancing wildly, gently moving, singing, drawing inventions, 60-second workouts, or cleaning.

5. Find listeners in your life and set dates for a "listening sessions of empathy & mirroring." The 60-second "listening sessions" are quite rewarding and not too taxing on your time or your listeners' efforts. Sounds odd? But once you explain yourself and offer the same to them, it will be a perfect 2 minutes for both of you.

6. This morning, before anyone else was awake I stepped outside and fed our pets, watered plants, and breathed in the morning air with several Qigong exercises.

7. Then I strolled on to our grassy yard. I laughed, talked kindly to plants, animals, imaginary faeries, and listened to the birds wake-up.

8. After these four minutes, I sat at my computer and created a politically positive message about supporting humane causes and becoming empowered to protest unkind political actions.

9. After these three minutes, I stood and finished a 10-minute Qigong movement meditation.

Inner Peace with Random Acts of Kindness - RAK

1. Spontaneously or quickly plan a moment of giving.

2. Plan to do a RAK sometime during your day, something very simple.

3. Plan to give someone something which you hope will improve their day.

4. Inspire yourself by visiting Kindness.org to absorb the generosity of others and do your bit too.

5. I wrote Thank You Notes to leaders of charities and donated $20 to five of them.

6. I gave my neighbor's grandkids baking goods.

7. I spoke with a suicidal teen and parent for some time while volunteering on a hotline.

8. I donated one of my paintings to a charity fundraiser.

9. I organized and cleaned good clothing for Salvation Army.

Inner Peace Body Work and Physical Sensations

Smell - Lavender, Pine, Mint, Cut Grass, Flowers

Stretch 60 seconds with Yoga, Pilates, Isometrics, Warm-ups

Hug others, pets, and self — with respect

Sigh Deeply and Practice Rhythmic Breathing Techniques

Dance specific steps or carefree movements with or without music

Rapid cardiovascular moments such as jumping jacks

KISS yourself, pets, inanimate object, lover, child, parent, friend

Take a Nature Walk in a Park or around a block

Gently Jog

Touch plants

Go barefoot

Hum, Whistle, Whisper, Laugh, and Sing

Smile!

Watch the clouds play with the sun's rays.

Watch how the water shines like diamonds.

Enjoy a Sunset on YouTube

For a quick meditation with sunsets, check out **https://www.youtube.com/watch?v=G0YotTZzPJo** *for a 3-minute mediation I've prepared just for you.*

Last night, I paused everything and called my family down to share the five-minute sunset together while sipping some warm apple cider.

This afternoon, I took a five-minute walk when the rain stopped to feel the Fall leaves mushy on the ground and smell the wet soil. While walking, I hummed, whispered a silly verse, and smiled. Then I ran like a child into the leaves and laughed.

 Tonight, I painted a sunset over the calm Pacific Ocean.

Absorb the brilliance of a sunset and become your own beautiful version of nature's best.
Dr. Carol Francis

Checklist of Tools Offered in Chapter 4

Check off those tools you wish to use today that match your style from Chapter 4.

_____ 1. Use audio meditations or zen-zone audios provided at AbuseTraumaRecovery.com/HealthCareWorkersTraumaRecovery/Inner Peace

_____ 2. Practice the ZEN ZONE MEDITATION MOMENT provided in this chapter 2-10 minutes a day or more.

_____ 3. Practice a Meditation of Humane Grief as exemplified

_____ 4. Practice one or more of the Nine Inner Peace Conversations provided

_____ 5. Practice one or more of the Nine Inner Peace with Random Acts of Kindness – RAK

_____ 6. Practice one or more of the Fourteen Inner Peace Body Works and Physical Sensations

_____ 7. Witness a sunset or sunrise, moonset, or moon rise.

Chapter 5
Recovery of Daily Home Life Demands

Life's Normal Demands

Typically, after short or long durations of emergencies or traumatic events, individuals become disorganized in daily life tasks. Clothes are unwashed and unfolded. Trash stacks up. Dishes are unclean. Cars are filthy. Bed sheets unchanged. Bills unpaid. Grass not mowed. Children neglected. Friendships ignored. Spouses unheeded.

All daily chores or everyday relationships are pushed to the side when urgent events must take priority. Overtime work, double/triple shifts, and exhausting schedules sidetrack normal living necessities. Physical fatigue, emotional exhaustion, and mental flooding leave nothing left for daily, ordinary demands.

When recovering from the demands of trauma work, we find ourselves now overwhelmed with unsolved problems at home, unfinished tasks, irritating chores, desk clutter. We have odd conflicts with loved ones who need loving attention. You are exhausted, yet ordinary demands piled-up in your absence.

In order to recover from your trauma work, you will need to rest and recalibrate your body's physical needs (Chapter 3). Next, you will need to practice simple restorative inner peace exercises (Chapter 4) that help you regain mental and emotional space for recovery. Then, you will need to pay attention to the chores of daily life that you have left unattended (Chapter 5).

Here in Chapter 5, we will walk you through step-by-step ways of resolving these "nagging" chores. Pick-up the pieces of your "normal" life. Reorganize daily life that has become chaotic.

Fortunately, resolving daily ordinary problems will help you 1) clear up the emotional clutter of normal life messes, 2) re-integrate you back into your daily homelife and identity, and 3) repair damage created by neglect, exhaustion, and distractions associated with your work with trauma.

First Steps

Five steps below will help you deal with your homelife demands:

1. Be patient with yourself.
2. Take each day and each day's tasks, one step at a time.
3. Use the procrastination tools provided in this chapter that motivate you or help you regain your daily functions.
4. Clearly, communicate with your family and friends about your *level of stress, fatigue or exhaustion.* This will help them comprehend what steps you are taking to recover and why you need to pace yourself.
5. Communicate with your family and friends *your plans for recovery.* Tell them your plans to so they can a) help you recover, b) be patient with you, c) anticipate that their lives too will return to normalcy. Let them read Chapters 6 and Chapter 7 as well.

Second Steps

Now, we will give you four tools to motivate your otherwise demotivated energies to get some chores done.

Daily tasks may look too big, too foreboding, or too boring. After all, worklife is horribly demanding, and the last thing you want to do is more work at home. You want home life to be a refuge. Yet, homelife has chores too. Family has desires and needs too. Frustrating isn't it, especially when you are recovering from trauma work.

We will begin with the "Just-Get-It-Done" approach.

Mental Attitude Trick #1: The "Just-Get-IT-Done" Mantra

"Just-Get-IT-Done" can become your mental declaration that leads you to finish those tasks, which are staring you in the face.

"Just-Get-IT-Done" can become a mantra. Mantras are meaningful words or phrases we repeat throughout our day which aim to steer our attitudes, emotions, and actions.

"Just-Get-IT-Done NOW!" becomes an answer to yourself any time you feel inclined to:

1) Procrastinate
2) Delay
3) Avoid
4) Pass-it-on to someone else to do

"Just-Get-IT-Done" becomes the coach on your shoulder shouting in your ears to ACT NOW.

Typically, after you begin your task, having coerced yourself with **"Just-Get-IT-Done,"** you feel less burdened, you feel more productive and organized, and you also enjoy hanging out with your new proactive self.

So, this "**Just-Get-IT-Done**" mantra is one of many tools you can use to help you resolve or finish whatever is stopping you.

Mental Attitude Trick #2: "Get Your Ass in Gear, Dude"

Some individuals wisely hassle themselves or "yell-at" themselves when they need to tackle something.

Wisely hassle them selves?

Yes. Sometimes.

We occasionally have to become irritated with our selves enough to kick us into action. Irritation can motivate us to finish washing dishes, pay bills, make appointments, or complete daunting projects. We wisely can use our agitated or angry feelings to motivate us when we are stalled, avoiding something, or feeling confused or indecisive.

Those people who function best "in the last-minute," use stress to wake up their brains and focus their efforts and time. Yes, procrastinators wake-up under pressure too. People with ADHD diagnoses often do their last-minute accomplishments in a harried state. When they are rushed, a task gets done. Then, they flow back to their "chill zone."

We respond quickly when we are in a crisis. Trauma work can train your body and mind to only respond when there is an emergency and be passive when nothing is urgent. This can make ordinary homelife chores harder to do because they may not seem urgent. "Get Your Ass in Gear, Dude" is a mental way of tricking your brain and body into action even when there is no emergency.

So, as you reintegrate back into your normal daily home routines, every so often you might decide to pressure yourself with a little self-kicking such as "Get Your Ass in Gear, Dude." Chances are you will feel better after you have gotten something done that was nagging at you.

Depression and Anxiety Due to Unresolved Daily Tasks

Individuals ask me to help them stop being panicked or anxious after a traumatic event. Interestingly, one of the dimensions of their panic or anxiety can be related to unresolved aspects of their ordinary lives. A normal unresolved issue is harassing them, making them feel very demotivated, agitated, irritable, or upset.

After they resolve those daily issues, a sweet calmness often settles into place. They feel internal conflicts and tensions gently soothing because they have solved the daily issues or finished the normal tasks hanging over their heads. For them, their agitation was a signal that something in their everyday life needed to get done.

Face it though, we all have unfinished projects or chores, all the time. If we live perpetually in a state of anxiety because something is not done, we will spiral into the cortisol-slaved-stress that kidnaps our body's health, our brain's clarity, and our inner peace.

Clearly, even after trauma work, we have to finish what we can in our homelife. Yet, we must be patient with our progress and energy levels. Practice our Inner Peace tools. Motivate ourselves to face dreaded chores. Grow our ability to function efficiently in our normal life, one step at a time.

Mobilize Normal Life with Seven Steps

Here are seven steps to use when you are unable to return to normal daily chores even after you have patiently rested, after you have carefully recuperated your physical well-being, and after you have rebuilt your emotional peacefulness. These seven steps will shift you from being inertly passive, checked-out, or depressingly vegging.

In this section, you will answer seven questions that help you focus on resolving and finishing distracting chores and projects.

Step One: What is not resolved in your life?

Identify your unresolved chores, projects, or irritants. Make a written list. Writing down your list is vitally important so that you do not have to keep rehearsing the list over and over again in order to remember all the pressing demands. Writing it down plucks it out of your brain so you do not have to be afraid of forgetting something. Write it down where you can always access the information. I love my "TO DO" application on my phone for this reason.

Step Two: What can I do to solve and finish this chore or project in my life quickly and efficiently?

Next, empower your thinking to **focus on solutions** to your chores, issues, or problems that are on your first list. Write *brief* descriptions of *easy* ways to finish the problems or to solve conflicts. You might have fun by listing crazy solutions, simplified solutions, and directly successful solutions.

Listing the crazy solutions enables you to start thinking outside your limiting brain. We can become crippled by thinking too small or thinking too complexly especially when we are stressed and overwhelmed. Thinking small or complexly can stop us from looking at enjoyably creative solutions or at simple, straightforward solutions.

KISS METHOD Mindset

The KISS METHOD means "Keep It Simple, Stupid!" or "Keep It Simple, Sweetheart." KISS is an affectionate way to remind yourself that there might be easy ways to fix things.

ASAP Mindset

For some people, most issues are simple to resolve merely by deciding to do the task ASAP - As Soon As Possible. **ASAP** saves people a lot of headaches caused by wasting time or procrastinating. Simply list those tasks that can be done NOW. Get as many off your list as you can, **ASAP**. Clear your brain, your list, and your schedule of simple tasks that you are dragging out. You are wasting wonderful mental energy on cluttering tasks that you can easily finish.

Of course, urgent tasks always are **ASAP**. Sometimes in life, you live from one **ASAP** to the next urgent **ASAP** at home. Parents of young children understand completely. For parents everything is *now* and there is little time for the more involved tasks, including sleeping!

Trauma work is also usually **ASAP** that can be efficient as well as stressful. At home we want the **ASAP** tasks to be efficient and motivating, especially since homelife tasks are not life-threatening usually.

Step Three: What steps do I need to take to resolve this?

Choose a solution from Step 2 and divide it into doable steps. Divide your solutions into doable subsections that will take less time to accomplish. This helps your tasks seem more manageable if you divide them into doable, multiple steps. If you can't put your mind around the whole project, divide the project into progressive steps that you can imagine getting done easily. Remember, write this solution-list down quickly and briefly. Don't make these lists another cumbersome task.

When you divide your tasks into small steps, make sure at least one of those small steps can be done today or very soon. Your immediate actions tell your brain two things:

1) You mean business and you will get it done
2) You are empowered to begin succeeding at resolving issues NOW.

Step Four: Do I need help resolving this?

Now pause a moment and **consider if you need help.** If a task seems overwhelming or not solvable, get some help. Maybe, you don't have the immediate expertise nor knowledge to solve the problem. You can decide that someone needs to help you who has the expertise.

Maybe you will need to have someone help you discover why you have mental blocks too. *Procrastinators Anonymous*, for example, might prove to be just the support system you need. Small groups who answer to each other also become tools to encourage your success.

Seek help when it is indicated. Other people can provide support, knowledge, skills, even the motivation that you need.

Step Five: What can I cross off my list today?

Cross off items on your list that are completely unnecessary to do. De-clutter your "TO DO LIST."

Also, cross-off the items on your list as you finish them. Crossing-it-off is a moment of satisfaction that is an easy one-second rewarding and motivating exercise.

Step Six: What is on my priority "to-do lists" and what is on my "wish-list?

Prioritize what "really matters" from those items that "would be nice if I could do it" items. This second group is a "wish list." *Items on your "wish list" do not need to be resolved.* "It would be nice to get that done" deserves a different emotional response from you then "I absolutely need to get this done." "Must get this done" needs to be matched with emotions of urgency or determination. "Wish I could" needs to be matched with desire and hope.

Make sure you practice matching the right emotional reactions to your priorities. Remember to practice being peaceful, not stressed-out, when you have items on your "wish list." "I want to" is a wishful pleasurable contemplation. "I gotta do it…" is a pressure-filled and motivating drive.

Step Seven: What do I need to finish today, and what do I need to follow-up on tomorrow?

Follow-up and **finish the tasks or steps reliably**. Being able to trust yourself to finish something brings satisfaction and peace to your relationship with your Self.

Self-Appreciation Moments

While you are being relentless in finishing your tasks or resolving your situations, practice self-appreciation. Refuel yourself with some personal verbal praise. Refresh yourself with quick rewards. Pause to appreciate your finished tasks. Share your success with a person who understands your efforts to recover from trauma work.

Be sure to respect yourself, reward yourself, and recuperate yourself. You have been dedicated to the well-being of others under very harsh circumstances. No doubt you want to rest. No doubt you want some self-indulgent rewards for working so hard. Therefore, each time you tackle and succeed at a task, shower yourself with *emotional self-respect* and a little reward that doesn't derail your progress. Also, plan time for resting or recuperating that you still may need as you are recovering from your trauma work and as you rebuild your stamina for your daily life activities.

Get Off Your Turtle

Finally, as you return to your normal life's routines and demands, remember to NOT use any time-wasting, complicated, or effort-intensive methods for completely your daily chores. Get off your slow, inefficient turtle pace of getting chores done.

Life is too short to take the long and slow approach to tasks that do NOT warrant that much effort. My drawings below remind me to get off the "slow turtle" when finishing a task especially when I can be effectively fast instead. Remember to use your energies and actions so that you can have more room for yourself for more important activities such as sleep, laughter, love, creativity, and living, which is what Chapter 6 is about.

Checklist of Tools Offered in Chapter 5

Check off those tools you wish to use today that match your style today and those tools you will use in the future.

_____ 1. I want to do the five parts of the First Step.

_____ 2. I want to do the Second Step.

_____ 3. I like the mindset of "Just-Get-It-Done"

_____ 4. I like the mindset of "Get Your Ass in Gear, Dude"

_____ 5. I like the mindset of "ASAP."

_____ 6. I like the mindset of the "KISS Method."

_____ 7. I choose to use the Seven-Step Strategy to tackle tasks.

_____ 8. I choose to list all the tasks I need to do for homelife.

_____ 9. I will look for simple, quick solutions for tasks.

_____10. I will create small steps for tasks that seem foreboding.

_____11. I will seek help without undue hesitation.

_____12. I will prioritize the "needs" from the "want" tasks.

_____13. I will plan today's and tomorrow's "to do" list.

_____14. I will practice Self-Appreciation.

_____15. I will Get off My Turtles and be efficient and quick.

Get Off Your Turtle!

Chapter 6
Increasing Your Energy

Repairing damage done to your physical well-being is our first priority discussed in Chapter 3. Next, we describe ways to cultivate your lost inner peacefulness. *Being present* for spontaneous moments of peacefulness is combined in Chapter 4 with a hundred tools teaching you also to *create* your inner peaceful moments. In Chapter 5, when you are relatively ready, we ease you back into your normal chores and typical daily life routines. In Chapter 6 we explore ways to reinvigorate your body, your mind, your emotions, and your spirit.

Energy Grows Incrementally and Cyclically.

Let me explain how all the tools in this book are designed to help you invigorate yourself incrementally and cyclically.

After Chapter 4, you may have thought that *inner peace* resembles a silent, meditating Tibetan Monk with closed eyes, gentle grin, slowed heartbeats, in a lotus posture. Yes, this is inner peace, one form of inner peace.

Inner peace also occurs when that same Tibetan Monk invigorates his/her life. That peaceful Monk also is exercising, walking, helping others, teaching, cleaning, traveling, laughing, protecting nature, eating wisely, defecating, sleeping, praying deeply, studying, earning livings, paying bills, raising families, fighting causes, dying for freedom, and marching for liberation.

The Tibetan Monk can meditate deeply in part because he/she is also very active at other times of the day. Also, the Monk can be highly productive because he/she is meditating deeply. Activity contributes to inner peaceful practices. Conversely, inner peaceful practices build energy for activities.

Cycles of Progress

Recognize that everything heals and grows in a Cycle of Progress.

When you cultivate your body's health (Chapter 3) and become more invigorated (Chapter 6), you will also have more inner peace (Chapter 4). You also will feel more inclined to finish daily tasks (Chapter 5). And as you grow your inner peace (Chapter 4) and finish more daily tasks (Chapter 5), you will feel more energized (Chapter 6) which makes your body healthier (Chapter 3).

Notice the *Cycle of Progress in your Recovery work.*

Yes, everything in you responds in a cyclical fashion. You will be rebuilding and improving one aspect of yourself, and it will help you rebuild other aspects of your life. Everything will cyclically improve.

Remember when I suggested that you need to drink water, eat quality vegetables and proteins even if you don't feel like doing it? Eventually, you will crave the healthy foods you once forced yourself to eat. Remember when I advised you go to bed at the same time for at least 2 weeks even if you don't feel sleepy? Eventually, you will be tired at that bedtime and restfully sleep a whole night. Remember those mental tricks you can use to start and finish tasks? Those mental tricks didn't include "do it if you feel like it" because you may not feel like it? Eventually, you will feel so good finishing your chores efficiently that you won't have to drag yourself to start them.

Good feelings are likely to follow good actions, not the other way around during Recovery.

As you begin to improve, small step by small step, healthy step by health step, worthy action by worthy action, you will begin to feel that all the other aspects of you begin to mend, rebuild, restore and eventually recover.

The Cycle of Progress occurs in all aspects of life. You know this already because you watch patients mend, rebuild, restore, and recover in this same progressive step-by-step cycle. The only time this does not occur is when an individual is moving toward their death.

You are moving toward recovery, not death.
So, step into your cycle of progress actively.

Remind yourself that you are moving toward recovery, especially on those discouraging, low energy, "I'm not doing so good" days. Yes, you will ebb and flow in your recovery. Yes, your overall recovery process will progressively improve, cyclically.

It would be wonderful if you felt energized first. The other healthy steps would seem easy to tackle. Unfortunately, that is not the way we typically expect to recover. Usually, the progress is synergistic, progressive, cyclical, and interdependent. Sometimes you have energy, making life easy, and other times you don't. Sometimes you are motivated emotionally, and other times you aren't. Rely more on taking actions that build energy and build motivation instead of waiting for energy and motivation to suddenly appear.

You will restore your energy levels incrementally. To help you reinvigorate, first remember what it feels like to have energy.

How Does Vigor Feel?

Recall feeling invigorated. Lively. Being peppy. Having optimism.

After trauma, abuse, or trauma work, our vigor is usually quite low. Our physical health is compromised. Our inner peace is lost. Our daily life is more chaotic and out-of-control. Our health care work has exhausted us emotionally, mentally, physically and spiritual. As a consequence, we can even forget what it once felt like to be energized. We are too fatigued and used-up to feel alive. During trauma work, we have been running on adrenaline and emergency pressures, not energy.

Emotional vigor is the opposite of depression.
Mental vigor is the opposite of mental fog or mental sluggishness.
Physical vigor is the opposite of fatigue and exhaustion.
Spiritual vigor is the opposite of hopelessness, nothingness, pessimism, and dread.

Emotional vigor is associated with laughter, love, enjoyment, excitement, enthusiasm, purposefulness, hopefulness, eagerness, inner peacefulness, feeling alive.

Mental vigor is associated with clear thinking, being alert, good memory, fast learning, efficient problem-solving, logical thinking, reasonableness, organized thoughts, and the ability to concentrate or pay attention.

Physical vigor is associated with endurance, muscular coordination, balance, staying awake during normal hours, desires, libido, appetite, affection, waking-up rested, keeping up with chores and daily demands, feeling capable of doing a task with no dread or fatigue.

Spiritual vigor is associated with feeling purposeful, feeling capable of being kind or empathic or compassionate when indicated, or passionate about causes even if angrily so. Experiencing your empowerment, faith in yourself, and faith in Divinity to create positive outcomes is also related to spiritual vigor. Your creative expressions and activities also reflect your spiritual vigor. Transcendent Inner Peacefulness (described in my book **Own Your Peace**) is also spiritual vigor.

Creating Inner Peace Invigorates

Since everything cyclically helps improve every other aspect of your recovery, let's look at how all that we have discussed in this book so far will enhance your energy, improve your vigor.

First, let's look at how Inner Peace INVIGORATES.

Inner peace does the following for your emotions:
- ➢ Eases your day's strains
- ➢ Calms your night's sleep
- ➢ Relaxes your knotted muscles
- ➢ Soothes your anger
- ➢ Fuels your compassion
- ➢ Inspires your humane actions
- ➢ Refreshes your attitudes

Inner peace does the following for your cognition:
- ➢ Enhances your concentration
- ➢ Focuses your attention
- ➢ Organizes your thoughts
- ➢ Channels your creative thoughts and talents into creations

Inner peace does the following for your physiology:
- ➢ Regulates your heartbeats
- ➢ Restores your muscles
- ➢ Harmonizes your skeleton-muscular structures and actions
- ➢ Evens out hormonal fluctuations

> Assists neurotransmitters which regulate your moods, thoughts and actions

> Pauses you right before a sudden adrenal burst which is needed for emergencies

> Takes over after extreme exertions or trauma-fatigue

Inner peace supports your brain and body functions throughout your days effectively. Inner peace connects you to your etheric body's energy fields and balances your chakra energy centers. Inner peace is inner consciousness that pervades all passive and active moments of your life, at all three depths: Serendipitous, Self-Created and Transcendent Levels. (Discussed at length in my book, **Own Your Peace: KISS Method for Inner Peaceful Living)**

Inner peace, in these ways, invigorates you to live, to act, to feel, to be all you can be in the moment.

These are reasons why you want to improve your Inner Peace which Chapter 4 helps you do. Return to practicing your Inner Peace skills to feel more alive, happy, eager, and satisfied with life.

Clinical Diagnoses and Therapy

Up to this point, I haven't actually discussed the possibility that your trauma work may have catapulted you into clinically diagnoseable mental health concerns.

Of course, PTSD and STS are mental health concerns. Compassion Fatigue and Professional Burnout are not considered mental health concerns. Yet, long term chronic trauma work or severely acute trauma work can shift our mind, body, and emotions right into mental health concerns such as clinical depression, clinical anxiety, depersonalization, reactive psychoses, mania, panic attacks, phobias, or personality disorders. Here are a few to consider:

> Clinical Depression, Bereavement, SAD, Malnutrition, Being Abused or Traumatized, Postpartum Depression, Burn-out, Post-Traumatic Stress Disorder, Thyroid Disorders, Menstrual Cycle or Hormonal Complications, Loss of Testosterone, Lack of Exercise, Learned Laziness or Learned Procrastination, Learned Helplessness, Chronic or Acute Illness or Disease, Panic Attacks, Generalized Anxiety, Social Phobias, Paranoia, Bi-Polar Disorders, Schizophrenia, Avoidant Personality, Schizoid Personality, Borderline Personality, and so much more.

Also, some trauma recovery research indicates that immediately altering the neurotransmitters or stress hormones after a trauma exposure may actually reduce or eliminate your trauma reactions. Thus, pharmaceuticals may be indicated for you if advised by a well-trained trauma-informed medical doctor, psychopharmacologist, or psychiatrist. Take advantage of what medical science has discovered as soon as you sense such might be additionally helpful so that you do not experience a slump that simply would not be necessary to endure nor helpful for you to endure.

Seek Professional Help to Invigorate

Seek professional help if you suspect that you lack vigor due to physical illnesses or psychological factors. The correct diagnosis accompanied by the best collection of treatments is, of course, a seriously important self-care step to take that may help solve your low energy quickly or over time.

Get help ASAP. Do not hesitate out of shame, guilt, or pride.

Have someone help you move in the right direction if you lack all capacity to mobilize yourself. Some professionals you might consider would be Medical Doctors, Nutritionists, Naturopathic Doctors, Psychologists, or Psychiatrists. Once you are on the right path with professional assistance, you can more easily implement self-help tools which invigorate your body, your brain, your personality and your soul.

At AbuseTraumaRecovery.com/HealthCareWorkersTraumaRecovery you will find a complete course that will detail therapies that have proven helpful with trauma recovery as well. **Paths to Recovery After Abuse and Trauma** has a meaty chapter about therapies too. And of course, you can contact my team and me at TherapyCounselingCoaching.com.

Healthy Choices Energize and Invigorate

Remember, when you have no vigor or low energy, you may not "want" to do anything. Also, what you "want" may be completely "out-of-whack" if you are severely drained by family, work, or illness. At times like these, you *might not be able to trust* yourself to make decisions or take actions that are based on "wants" because your desires might be completely confused if you are fatigued or drained.

As a consequence, you may need to begin to take actions or intervene on your own behalf without the "want" or urge to act. You might have to act without having the emotional energy to change. You may need to act even if you don't feel like it. You may need to eat, even if you aren't hungry. You may need to exercise, even though you feel tired.

Without energy,

we tend to avoid doing what will create energy.

Exercise and Move to Invigorate

Move your body so you can cleanly sweat, channel adrenaline, stimulate endorphins, grow muscles, mobilize your metabolism, oxygenate, stir your blood, impact your bones positively. Push yourself optimally step by step into your next best efforts and success.

Start with a few minutes several times a day. Increase to 20-60 minutes per day.

Eat to Invigorate

Everything that goes into your body impacts your energy. Eating foods that are loaded with real energy will load you with real energy. Supplements such as vitamins, minerals, and amino acids can help as well. Herbal and green teas and oxygenated water keep you hydrated, cleansed, and electrically balanced.

Oh, you already know those foods that slow you down: sugar, processed foods, preservatives, caffeinated extremes. For some of you, carbohydrates such as breads, noodles, or rice are good for energy and for others, such makes you sluggish. For some of you, nuts, legumes or starches are amazing sources of energy and for others they are loaded with the wrong combinations. For some, a diet which includes sweet foods like fruits or natural sweeteners is essential for energy and for others those foods are like street drugs.

You have to find your:

1) Way of eating to feel great
2) What times of day to eat so you feel great
3) What foods make you feel fantastic in the moment or in the long term
4) What foods make you sleep well or what make you crash and drag

Also, for some, food is a source of inner peacefulness as they enjoy cooking, savoring flavors, experiencing textures, and soaking in smells that deeply impact their senses of well-being. Food for some stirs wonderful memories of family, travels, and home. Food for some is creative and divine.

Your energy formula regarding food may also change throughout your life based on age, exercise, hormonal changes, health issues, traumas, or demands at work or at home.

The goal is to use food as an energy source when you are trying to invigorate yourself.

Sleep to Invigorate

As with exercise and food, sleep is a tool that can invigorate an individual when there is

1) Enough sleep
2) Enough quality deep sleep
3) Reliable sleeping times that match your body's style, body's age, body's demands for the day or week, body's biorhythms

No one formula for sleeping patterns matches everyone, so you will have to experiment. Also realize, your need for sleep and the type of sleep you get will change during your week, months and years. I highly recommend using a device that measures the quantity and quality of sleep you are receiving nightly to guide your decisions about your sleeping patterns and sleeping needs.

In addition, you know that trauma work interrupts sleep cycles and sleeping schedules often. Adrenaline and cortisol are stress hormones that keep us alert and interfere with sleep. Horrible flashbacks, memories of events, guilt, worry, and despair keep us awake. Fretting about the next day disrupts our sleep cycle too.

Finally, trauma work disturbs the brain's neurochemistry, which would otherwise allow us to easily shut-off and sleep and then wake up refreshed. Our brains adapt to trauma, keeping us in hyper-alert emergency modes.

You will have to *retrain your body's cycles*. You will have to retrain or readapt your brain's chemistry. You will have to alter emotions that allow you to fall asleep, stay asleep, and wake up refreshed.

Please refer to Chapter 3 again for some sleeping tools or contact me as well to help you work through this aspect of renewing your energies and vigor with quality sleep.

Once again, listening to your style of sleeping that invigorates you and relaxes you is crucial.
Retrain your mind and body to sleep once again.

Energize your Personality

Below are suggestions for invigorating your personality.

Playfully engage weekly in fun and enriching activities that aim toward physical health, social positive fun, random acts of kindness, learning, inspirational thinking, and soulful reflection. (Examples: Frisbee Throwing, Cooking, Reading to Children, Group Meditations, Gifting Neighbors, Massages, Family Game Nights.)

Learn and do what really "turns you on" and makes you excited to be alive. Do at least a little of that "turn on" daily. (Gardening, Reading, Writing, Painting, Running, Sex, Cleaning, Auto Repair, Building, Inventing, Singing, Playing Piano.)

Surround yourself as much as possible with individuals who aim to live life with vigor, enthusiasm, optimism, empowerment, respect, and humane consciousness. (Going to a coffee shop while doing bills or writing emails is an example. Circulate in Meetups, Museums, Workshops, Classes, Theatre or Films with audience interactions, On-line interactive courses.)

Practice daily self-reflection. Invest in soulful or spiritual reflections that inspire you to move beyond the grind of daily chores. (Yoga, Journaling, Meaningful Art, Pithy Conversations.)

Be alert to the following Energy Drains to your personality:

➤ Negative people
➤ Burn-out with excessive work hours
➤ Burn-out with poor eating or poor sleep or lack of exercise

- Lack of emotional experiences
- Lack of socially invigorating experiences
- Too much time with socially or emotionally draining experiences.
- Too much routine
- Too little refreshing moments
- Too little worthwhile "downtime" moments
- Too much isolation
- Too little quiet time
- Demanding people
- Chores

Energize Your Brain's Functions to Invigorate

Keep your brain fueled with active tools such as Luminiosity or Sudoku. When desirable, let your brain rest and veg at other worthy times. Drink plenty of water and good brain-food for your neurological system as well, as already discussed.

Certain devices and apps are now available that support brain functions and brain entrainment. Consider the following.

Use Devices, Apps, and Scientific Tools to Invigorate

In this wonderful era of devices, I find there are certain electronic tools and App which help people stay alert, attentive, focused, and concentrated. These tools engage our brains. They keep us connected to loved ones or the world. They make us be proactive or impassioned.

They can stir and inspire us. They can calm us. They can give us moments of fun, happiness or ease.

Yes, technology is often accused of keeping us detached, overwhelmed, distracted or dehumanized. All advances have positives and negatives. Here, I wish to emphasize their positive benefits.

These following tools aim to produce states of mindfulness, meditations, mind control, anger management, anxiety management, assistance with insomnia, focus, concentration, and transcendent mind-soul activities. Devices I find quite useful include BrainTap, Wild Divine/Unyte, Neurosky, Epoc Emotiv, Epoc Insight, Muse, HeartMath EmWAVE, Mindflex, EffEmmit, NeoRhythm, TMS, Halo, MindValley Meditation App, Kaiser Permanente's Calm, and Headspace App.

I recently provided a seminar for one of these very helpful devices, Muse. The Muse device and its apps help individuals with anxiety reduction, mental distraction, meditation or mindfulness practices. With their permission, Muse has provided the link (below) so that you can watch this seminar for free. You will learn about its applications and become familiar with this consumer-grade neurobiofeedback tool. Here is the link:

https://attendee.gotowebinar.com/register/453875030276 8526081

Neurosky has more usable applications at the time of this publication than Muse and is relatively easy to use as well. It is less comfortable on your head. Neurosky is also great for children. With children, I also use neurobiofeedback toys such as Mindflex which is quite similar to Neurosky but uses actual balls and objects moved solely by your brainwaves. These are fun and very instructive devices.

Epoc's Emotiv and Insight are more sophisticated neurobiofeedback tools that have more software, more Human-Computer Interface (HCI) research, and has both consumer and research-grade equipment. I use these EEG headsets with my research groups associated with reducing depression, reducing learned helplessness, enhancing happiness, and bio-identification discoveries.

Unyte (formerly Wild Divine) is a colorful, playful, and usable biofeedback system that uses HCI in its software applications. Unyte is wonderfully capable of teaching individuals how to concentrate, focus, breath peacefully, regulate their heart, or calm their skin's perspiration. These biofeedback tools interface with spiritual concepts, mindfulness practices, or meditation tools as well. I will use this, along with all the other devices I am mentioning here, to help with anxiety, depression, insomnia, and attention difficulties as well.

HeartMath EmWave is the easiest of biofeedback tools that I carry with me, along with Muse and BrainTap to demonstrations all the time. HeartMath EmWave has considerable research helping trauma survivors and PTSD patients recover. EmWave is a small device that has helped soldiers and trauma survivors remember what it is like for their body, heart, breathing, and mind to return to

Parable of the Simple

"So simply," said Master Staejung

"Destructiveness destroys reliably.

Constructiveness constructs, most definitely.

Compassion stirs kindness unquestionably.

Ascension tools breed ascension experiences.

Practices of peacefulness stir Inner Peace.

So Simple."

Chapter 7
Family and Friends
During Your Recovery Process

Human relationships can be easy and complicated. You and others can be supportive and demanding. You and others can be uplifting and depleting.

People can be understanding and judgmental. We can be calming and aggravating. We might be enlightened and foolish. Respectful and abusive. Empathic and critical. Generous and self-centered. Informed and clueless.

You and others in your life might be conversational or nonverbal. Be good listeners or inattentive. Be helpful or needy. Be good problem-solvers or problem-makers. Be capable of enduring hardship or easily defeated.

I have no way of knowing how your family members treat you on a regular day. Do you know their styles, their strengths, their needs, their wants? Do you know how they experience your style, strengths, and needs?

Also, I do not know how they respond toward you when you are preoccupied with work worries. Do you know how they feel for you and think about you during those times? Do you know how they cope with their wants and their needs when you are emotionally unavailable for them and for the relationship? Are they equipped to help you through your recovery or likely to interfere with your recovery process? Can any of your family members or friends be relied upon to provide a wise listening ear? Can they generously provide patience, supportive space, and time to regroup?

Can they understand, constructively, the stress of your work? Do they appreciate the value of your professional skills? Are they tuned-in to the urgency of each trauma work experience? Do they believe in your purpose and work-related decisions? Do they support your risk-taking commitments?

On the other hand, have you been neglectful of any family members or friends during your taxing time at work? Have you needed them to seek other people to fulfill their relationship desires? Have you expected your family and friends to be supportive of you but failed to be equally supportive of them?

You too can be complicated and easy to be around. You can be wonderful and problematic. You too can be generous and selfish. Part of your recovery work will require you to repair the damage that has eroded in your relationships when you were distracted, unavailable, or neglectful due to your own human limitations. You will need to repair damages caused by your prioritizing stressful work over home life relationships.

One thing I do know, each of your family members or close friends has been adversely impacted by your trauma work as well. They have had to sacrifice their desire to spend quality time with you. They have had to live their life's activities and progress without your highly involved presence while you were invested in trauma work and resting-up for your next tough shift as well. Potentially, they have been seriously exposed to dangerous viruses or deadly bacteria you brought into the house, transmitted through your body and clothing.

Consider also, that the many adversities in the lives of your family members or friends were likely minimized. Their needs often took a backseat to what you were assisting elsewhere. Moreover, they were likely hurt, saddened, discouraged, even offended by your lack of love, attention, appreciation, celebration, and vigor.

Based on the realization that I DO NOT know how supportive your family members and friends are now, during your recovery, and based upon the realization that I also DO NOT know how much they have been adversely impacted by your trauma work, I will make the following recommendations. I realize, once again, that not all of these recommendations will fit your situation nor fit your relationships. As always, please begin with what might work today or this week. Then shift to other interventions as everyone progresses over time and effort.

Take Time for Relationship Inventory

The first exercise I would recommend for you at this point is to write down answers to the following questions so that you can gain perspective about your relationships and how you will need to fuel your relationships to become healthy and recovered as well.

Answer these questions about the significant family members and main friends in your life:

1. How do I need this person to support me during my recovery?
2. What strains did I place on them during my preoccupation with trauma work?
3. What "broke-down" in this relationship because of my preoccupations?
4. How does this person need me to help them during their recovery from my trauma work too?
5. What specific strengths and weaknesses does this person have to deal with my trauma work and its impact on their personal well-being?
6. What helps this person feel appreciated, loved, visible, valued, and connected to me?

7. What communication skills do we both have to create doable solutions that strengthen our relationship?
8. What strengths do I have to keep our relationship healthy and growing both while I am recovering and during my professional trauma work?

Consider Educating Your Family and Friends

When I wrote my book **Reintegrating Soldiers with Families,** I included chapters written for the family members as they too suffered Secondary Trauma Stress related to the absence of their deployed soldier and related to the return of their traumatized soldier. Some chapters of this book, **Recovery After Trauma Work,** can likewise be shared with your family members. In fact, this whole book might help them understand what your recovery process might include.

Also, I recommend that each family member or friend of trauma survivors take some of the Courses offered at *AbuseTraumaRecovery.com* so they can better understand and help the recovery process. In like manner, your family members and friends can access all the Courses you have signed up for as well at *AbuseTraumaRecovery.com/HealthCareWorkersTrauma Recovery.*

Often, I have family counseling sessions that focus upon what the traumatized individual has endured more clearly. We also discuss how the family members can best support the recovery process for the survivor. In a similar manner, feel free to organize family counseling sessions that help those who love you so they can better understand your situation and also understand how they can help.

Additionally, these sessions can help each family member describe how they have been adversely impacted by your professional trauma work. They can also describe what they need in order to heal and recover as well. Moreover, these sessions can help family members cultivate loving feelings, avenues of communication, and resolutions for mounting problems ignored during these hard times.

Consider Organizing Your Plans for Your Recovery with Your Home Team

Before each shift, health care workers are briefed and debriefed about the needs of patients, residents, equipment, protocols, and staffing. Consider using this same technique with your family members and friends. Daily or weekly, have each member describe 1) what they have experienced, 2) what they need, 3) what they anticipate, 4) what will be the plan of action for the day or week, and 5) what will be the solutions to problems faced.

Build Teamwork Skills in Your Family Structure

Ideally, you would have already trained your friends and family members to be 1) problem-solvers, 2) communicators, and 3) team players. But I am a realist, and I recognize that most families have not taken the time to organize their family team effectively.

If children, partners, siblings, or parents have not been taught to be responsible toward the household needs and function like a quality team member within the family, it is hard to begin to impose such structures or tools when you are in the middle of trauma work or recovery.

Nonetheless, you may need to begin to teach teamwork skills including 1) communication skills, 2) organizational skills, 3) responsibility skills, and 4) teamwork consciousness. This may be the essential work of your recovery with your family and friends.

Create Respect When You Express Yourself

CREATE RESPECT during each communication you extend, in each request you make, and during each lesson you teach. Avoid sounding or being authoritarian. Avoid angry demands since such makes every human-being at any age resentful, resistant, and uncooperative. You know how broken it is when a health care worker is disrespectful, bossy, rude or condescending. So, don't replicate that broken approach at home even if you are tired, cranky, or at wits-end.

Write-Out Your Plans for Recovery

Often, not always, family members and friends respond better to succinct lists you write that help them understand your plans for recovery. Consider this technique as being similar to a grocery list, a recipe, or calendar entry of events shared by the whole family or group.

This plan that you list for your family members and/or friends needs to be 1) simple, 2) easy to read, 3) functional not emotional, 4) forward thinking with clear objectives and goals, 6) void of all BLAME and CRITICISMS, and 7) focused on what you will be doing daily to recover.

Ask Your Family or Friends to List Their Needs

Next, you can request a brief conversation with your family members or friends to discuss what they will need from you once you have recovered sufficiently.

Ask them for a list of 3-5 items they wish you to address, once you have recovered, that you can include in your list of goals. Ask them to be specific, clear, and unemotional as well. Ask them to avoid blame and criticism. Ask them to describe what they look forward to experiencing during your future together.

Empathically View Your Family and Friends

Of course, not all family members or friends will be able to follow through as objectively and positively as you would prefer. Understandably, they might be harboring resentments that you prioritized others above them. They likely feel hurt by your absence, even neglected. Reasonably, they could be feeling distant and not eager to be connected with you yet again anticipating that you will only disappoint them or neglect them again and again.

You will need to recognize their perspectives, their desires, their needs, and their own Secondary Traumatic Stress. They _will_ have STS to your trauma work similar to what a soldier's family experiences. This is also similar to what your patients' family endures as well when the patient returns home to recover. You are not alone in this struggle to reconnect while you are also recovering.

Being empathic and understanding to your family and friends' reactions to your ordeal might be very hard for you as you are depleted and exhausted. Nonetheless, providing as much emotional concern for their reactions and needs typically (not always) helps them 1) feel valued, 2) feel understood, 3) feel hopeful that their wants and needs will be addressed, 4) feel like they are among your team players, and 5) feel reconnected to the relationship that exists between you and them. These are five very important relationship emotions you will want to create as much as possible.

Add to these conversations (and to your list) easy-to-do activities that will address at least one of their items

111

on their list. *You must absolutely, reliably follow-through on these activities with the same commitment you would have to a patient or resident, or you will seriously hurt your loved-one and harm the relationship further.*

Keep Your Family Members and Friends Informed about Your Recovery Progress

Simply and easily keep your family and friends informed about how you are progressing. This type of informative conversation is to be minimally emotional, and very appreciative and constructive. No blame, no criticism, no extreme emotional brokenness is to be expressed during these very simple updates. Ideally.

Choose Your Compassionate Confidante Carefully

Other conversations with family and friends can be emotional and part of your healing if they agree to participate in helping you cathart your emotions and relive your memories.

Choose carefully who among your friends and family members can endure your catharsis and remain compassionate. Not everyone you love or know is equipped for deep conversations or sharing about traumatic experiences. Some family members and friends are best for sharing fun moments, laughter and humor. Others are best for interesting entertainment. Others are best objective problem-solvers. Others need you more than you need them. Choose your team carefully based upon what their emotional skills are and what their time constraints are as well.

Consider Diverting Your Needs to Counseling Sessions

Recognize also that your needs may exceed the skills and capacities of any of your family or friends. If so, consider counseling or psychotherapy. Such private and confidential professional space may be needed in order for you to cathart deeply, explore complexly, or breakdown fully emotionally at times.

Counseling or psychotherapy may provide you with essential healing conversations, insights, and emotional processing which your family and friends cannot provide or do not provide. When these types of needs are met by your therapist or counselor, it will be easier to engage with your family and friends about other topics and in other circumstances with more mental balance and emotional flexibility.

Counseling can unburden your playful moments. Therapy can free you to be more carefree with family and friends. Such can help you have the mental and emotional space to be more empathic and giving to family and friends as well.

Relationships are Vulnerable During Trauma and Trauma Recovery

All relationships can be destroyed. All relationships have certain fragility. All relationships are breakable. Do not take any relationship for granted. Anyone who cares about you or needs you, or wants your time and attention, will also be adversely impacted by your focus on trauma work and by your need to recover from that trauma work too. Any neglect, disproportionate burdens, one-sidedness, verbal dumping, or distancing will harm your connection. Your connection will need to be repaired accordingly. Do not fool yourself about these facts.

Prioritize Your Teams Carefully

Therefore, as much as possible, prioritize your primary relationships and how you wish those relationships to grow and be healthy.

Answer these questions.

1.What does each of your relationships need to grow and to be healthy?

2. What do the other people in your relationships need from you or want with you?

Perhaps you will choose to not participate in future trauma work because you wish to protect, prioritize, and grow your primary relationships more than you need to participate in future trauma work.

If you are in a family or have primary relationships, you might wish to view these as teams that you are on. Any decisions, therefore, would need to be made as team players. Decisions you make about your work become part of the team's experiences and part of the team's growth or destruction. As a team member, not as an isolated independent person, your decision is the team's decision.

Your career goals, your financial commitments, your time away from the relationships, your emotional and mental preoccupations away from the relationships all impact the teams you are on. If the teams are your priorities, your decisions will need to reflect such in order to keep the teams healthy and thriving. There is no other way to function on a team.

Often families and friends break when they are not treated as fragile, not treated with the necessary respect, and not viewed as teams that need to make team-related decisions. So be aware of which teams you are truly prioritizing and how you are building or harming those teams' well-being with each independent decision you decide to implement.

Checklist of Tools Offered in Chapter 7

In Chapter 7 we have explored many different ways to work with your family and friends during recovery. Check off those tools you wish to use today or in the future.

_____ 1. Answer the 8 questions on the "Relationship Inventory" about your friendships and family members.

_____ 2. Consider educating your family and friends by providing them parts of this book or all this book.

_____ 3. Consider providing an objective list of your recovery plans for this week or month to your family and friends.

_____ 4. Consider asking your family members and friends for the list of their 3-5 wants or needs they have of you after you recover or during your recovery.

_____ 5. Consider building teamwork skills within your family.

_____ 6. Consider how to communicate with respect to your family and friends.

_____ 7. Plan to empathically listen to your family and friends in terms of their needs, wants, and trauma reactions.

_____ 8. Choose who will be your confidante carefully.

_____ 9. Consider counseling or therapy to address your recovery, emotionally and mentally.

_____ 10. Consider counseling or therapy for your family's recovery process.

_____ 11. View your family as a team you are on not as an obstacle, or as a group that needs to "put-up" with your trauma work.

_____ 12. Prioritize the teams you wish to invest time and energy into carefully.

_____ 13. Recognize that all teams are fragile, and that your teams will thrive only if you invest in their well-being since you are one of their team-players.

Chapter 8
Grieving Patients' Deaths

"Feels so helpless."
"I never feel okay with it."
"Words can't describe the feelings."
I don't want a patient to die when I'm gone."
"It feels like a gift if no one dies during my shift."
"I feel so sad and there is nothing I can do for them."
"You try and try, and patients will die no matter what.
"Sometimes I can't leave when my shift is done because
I can't sleep at night thinking about those who died
during my shift."

Death is not an experience to be neatly explained and tied into a pretty bow, as you well know. "End-of-life" discussions with patients and families are tough regardless of progression of age, disease, or pains. Everyone loses including all medical professionals irrespective of connection, rationalization, back stories, or belief systems.

So, be forewarned, in the next three chapters, we will not be making death a tidy issue. Your reactions to death and dying won't be minimized nor objectified.

Also know, as we discuss ways for you to manage your reactions to your patients' dying processes and to their deaths, that you will react uniquely based upon who you are today. In these three chapters, many tools will be offered. Select those tools today which help you:

- Understand your many tangled reactions
- Manage the ebb and flow of your messy emotions
- Cope with intruding thoughts, nightmares or worries
- Return you to living your life fully
- Develop your own strategies for future professional encounters with patients' deaths

Ebbs and Flows of Painful Grief

When your patient begins the dreaded descent toward death, you may resonate empathically entering into your own grief cycle as well. When a patient dies, your grief swells.

Painful feelings likely surge through your body first as your biochemistry and neurology metabolizes your patient's death. Intensity of your body's surge then swells for minutes, perhaps subsides, then swells and subsides cyclically. Your body cycles the sad news like ocean waves at the shoreline; it ebbs and flows.

Your physiology, of course, influences your thoughts, emotions, and actions. Then, all your systems ebb and flow reactively. Your thoughts, emotions and actions then impact your body's systems and vice versa. Grief loops. Grief involves all of who you are, physically, emotionally, mentally, spiritually, and socially.

Grief is therefore not a linear reaction. It swells. It subsides. It trickles out. It emerges slowly. It explodes. It lessens. It spontaneously erupts. It calms.

Riding Grief's Waves

Learning to ride the worst moments of grief is part of what you need to practice. Practice these suggestions when grief is triggered:

Breathe.
Whisper calming words to yourself.
Stroke your arms and head.
Cry.
Crying is an anti-depressant.
Wale.
Whimper.
Ask for hugs.
Give hugs.
Whisper your patient's name.
Light a candle.
Perform a ceremony.
Talk with your patient, even though they passed on.
Share grief with their families if appropriate.

Share grief with friends and colleagues you trust.
Know that you are grieving because you love.
Remember your gift of love to others.
Remind yourself that grief does ebb.
You will get a break.
Remind yourself that grief is physiological at first.
Ride that physical wave without fear and without
becoming rigid or repressive.
Feel, express, then release.
Feel again.
Express it again.
Release it again.
Reassure yourself that grief does subside.
Avoid shaming yourself for grieving.
Know that love and compassion also have grief involved.

Learning to allow yourself to refresh during those low grief moments is another practice. Chapter 9 will lead you to tools that help you ebb and flow fluidly through grief.

Gain more relief from the videos, audios and journal exercises offered free to all readers with the code **Recovery2020** at this link:

https://abusetraumarecovery.com/healthcareworkerstraumarecovery/

Grief Cycles

Grief triggers so many different painful reactions causing you to experience chaos, overwhelm, or confusion. Grief can flow into such intensity it triggers the urge to die.

At grief's height, it dismembers hope or courage. It stymies your willpower. Freezes your actions. Numbs your senses. It dominates all else.

Then, grief will ebb a bit or a lot, granting temporary respite. Appearance of normalcy returns until the cycle is triggered again.

This cycle can continue for years over loss of one's child or loving partner or a young parent. You will see this with your patients' families or in your own personal life.

Grief also is likely to linger longer or deeper whenever a death seems "premature," "shocking," or "wrongful." Often, the deeper the connection, the deeper and/or longer the grief cycles occur.

With your patients, your grief may last for a few hours, few days, maybe months. Yet, the grief will not remain the same intensity at its high points similar to how storms dissipate over time. Recovery from grief can "just take time." Grief gradually diminishes.

Odd, isn't it, how initial intense moments can slip into being emotional memories. Life forges forward. Humans adapt. You will adapt. Remember that too.

Chronic Exposure to Traumatic Deaths

During chronic and ongoing medical emergencies, such as the Covid19 Pandemic, grief builds and builds as more and more die painful and strange deaths.

Chronicity of deaths can kidnap healthcare workers into their own traumatic reactions. Secondary Traumatic Stress (STS) reactions can be induced by an overload of deaths.

STS grief is compounded by horrifying types of death too. Such deaths are "wrongful," "premature," "shocking," "unnecessary" and terrifying deaths. You, as a healthcare worker, will have your unique definitions as to what you feel is a "premature," "shocking," or "wrongful" deaths. Those will likely touch you deeper and impact you greater.

Also, some patients you will connect to meaningfully and others more functionally. The meaningful connections will likely touch you deeper. The painful cycles of grief likely will grip you more when you invest more. More compassion, more time, more skills, more worry, or more significance will accumulate into more grief when a patient dies.

Reread Chapter 2 about STS, a type of PTSD impacting healthcare workers. Chapters 8 and 9 address these STS-related *grief reactions* and how to recover from such.

Also, remember that I have very helpful videos, meditative audios, and journaling tools that you can access for free with this code **Recovery2020** at this link:

https://abusetraumarecovery.com/courses/course-1-how-traumatized-are-you/

Avoid Grief or Traverse Grief?

Should you avoid compassion for your patients in order to avoid grief?

I will suggest to you that learning how to beneficially traverse grief's ebbs and flows is more ideal than becoming distant, aloof, hardened or dark.

Thanks to Dr. Bernie Siegel, author of ***Love, Miracles, and Medicine***, we know beyond a doubt that your compassion helps patients live or endure better. Many researchers that he inspired empirically demonstrate that love-filled medical care helps surgeries, medicines and procedures beneficially. You can access one of my interviews with Dr. Siegel which will inspire you as a medical professional. Here is that podcast link to enjoy. Your heart will be encouraged to risk loving those who are dying too.

Driving this idea further, Dr. Larry Dossey author of *__Healing Words,__* challenges all practitioners to care. Dossey suggests that prayers impact healthcare. He noted that general prayers have the same statistical relevance to recovery as do pharmaceuticals. He proposed that perhaps it would be malpractice to not pray for our patients the same way not providing a pharmaceutical appropriately would be malpractice. Your love and your prayers impact your patients deeply.

Your emotional compassion aids bodily healing in your patients. Empirical research is clear. Your ability to provide excellent medical care alongside your dosage of compassion may prove pivotal to many people you treat throughout your career.

Is caring about your patient a burden then if you might have to endure grief when they die? Sure. Perhaps it is also an honor to grieve our fellow fragile human family.

What Medical Fields Suits Your Grief Tolerance?

Before answering this question for yourself, please allow yourself to be free of any shame, blame or guilt about whether you should deal with death and dying.

Many helpful medical procedures and fields deal with death very little. Perhaps currently, those arenas match your temperament and lifestyle much better. Perhaps you can intermingle your medical skills with compassion with minimal risk of grief.

You can decide if grief-related medical work is in your personal and professional best interest. Your style of caring for patients may not be suitable to trauma work, intensive care units, life and death diseases, or emergency room interventions. Some practitioners care deeply for each patient yet are unable to manage grief. Their patient's possible death is crushing. Perhaps, pediatric wellness-care suits your current style better than cancer wards or geriatrics.

Some healthcare workers are more stoic and not able to administer compassion at fragile times. Others are more strictly cognitively-oriented and likely to objectify patients, treatment, and end-of-life matters. Medical research and strict diagnostic work benefits from objective analysis more than hands-on treatment. Some say surgeons are better when they can objectify. Other research indicates that compassionate or empathic surgeons produce health-inducing attitudes more readily, before, during and after surgery.

Over time, some medical professionals become hardened or simply unwilling to maneuver through messy feelings such as compassion or grief. Chances are, these professionals have not learned what you are reading in this book about navigating deep emotions. Or, perhaps these healthcare workers need a break, a change, or easier emotional interactions.

Remember, harbor no shame or guilt when you decide if you wish to endure the death and dying aspects of your patient's care. Decide consciously and conscientiously.

Frankly, it appears that some practitioners, some personalities, are particularly suited to End-of-Life situations or capable of life and death related treatments. Enduring grief takes *grit, resilience, and perspective*. Likely, it is ideal if healthcare workers can feel that it is a "calling" to help patients' transition. We discover that nurses in the Hospice sectors particularly feel so called, and of course trained, to help families and patients face their end of life.

Even when self-selected, well-trained, and emotionally steadied to deal with inevitable deaths, healthcare workers face devastating moments. Mass shootings crushingly overwhelm hospitalists with "wrongful" deaths en masse. Battle zones or bombings result in mangled gore of tragic proportions.

Covid19 has flooded hospitals with horrific deaths in massive numbers. Covid19 understandably has overwhelmed practitioners' emotional readiness to handle such grief. Covid19 has also endangered health workers' lives and their families' well-being, adding additional levels of distress. Covid19 in the USA has also flooded healthcare workers with appallingly poor Federal necessary assistance. The STS reactions to Covid19 needs to be helped. As of the writing of this book, the Covid19 is the primary reason for creating this Recovery Program for Healthcare Workers, something which has been needed for decades.

Self-Reflection Moment

Let's do a moment of self-reflection before moving forward. Check-off those ideas below that currently describe you.

_____ 1. I feel like I have a calling to help people face the end of their life.

_____ 2. I have managed my grief well under all the circumstances I have faced so far, both personally and professionally.

_____ 3. I believe my compassion has combined with my medical professional skills with definite ease. For the most part, patients respond well to this combination.

_____ 4. I have noticed that I buffer myself from experiencing grief too deeply by buffering my involvement with patients. I do so by altering my work schedule, taking time off conscientiously, and using my free time wisely. I do not buffer my involvement by having less compassion for my patients, however.

_____ 5. I have a belief-system or paradigm that enables me to deal with death without losing my compassionate involvement and without experiencing crippling grief.

_____ 6. I grasp fully that grief is a transitory experience that has different intensities. I feel capable of riding the ebbs and flows of such grief without compromising my responsibilities and personal relationships.

How Your Grief Improves Your Healthcare Work

Now that we understand the ebb and flow of grief, let's now reframe Kübler-Ross's Five Stages of Grief to better understand your healthcare experiences. As you will recall from your schooling, Kübler-Ross suggested people weave in and out of five reactions when they find out they are dying or that someone has died. Recall her five stages of her Grief Cycle model:

Denial – Not possible, not me, no way, error, shock
Anger – So unfair, who's to blame, Why me
Bargaining – If I do this "thing," I can avoid death
Depression – Defeated, hopeless, helpless, despair
Acceptance – Making plans, settling affairs, sharing

We will now reframe Kübler-Ross' model so you can better use your many reactions as a healthcare practitioner. Yes, you read that right. You will learn how to use your grief to better care for your patients and yourself. As you read this section, underline all the reactions you currently recognize *as your own* in your healthcare practice.

Changing Your Perspective on Grief and Its Value to You and Your Patients

Each of Kübler-Ross's five grief reactions need to be reframed to help you understand the value of your grief responses. Once you understand the value of your grief to your patients and yourself, you will experience your emotional pain from these profoundly different perspectives.

Different perspectives about grief
help you manage its pain.

Value of <u>Denial</u> when the "Death Sentence" is Proclaimed

Denial of the "death sentence" actually:

- Motivates both patient and medical team to try harder
- Encourages being more experimental
- Encourages more diligent or conscientious work
- Exudes more hope

Hope, as we all know, is a crucial element of recovery for all patients. "I will be among the percentage

131

who recover!" is the proclamation of hope. This hope denies the relevance of any death sentence.

Faith too is relevant. If a patient has faith in a pharmaceutical, a medical procedure, or a surgeon's skill, they are more likely to recover faster, fuller and easier than patients who lack such faith. If a patient has faith in prayer's power and God's interventions, there is a higher percentage of recovery than with those lacking faith. The atheistic or agnostic commitment of scientific communities are puzzled by such, but the empirical data is solid.

It seems hope or faith modifies biochemistry by reducing stress hormones. Hope and faith enhance immune system functions. Hope and faith instruct (neurologically) the body's healing functions as well. These are all being further researched and are popularly described by Dr. Bruce Lipton in his book ***Biology of Belief***. Minimally, hope and faith have the placebo effect that clearly does support the body's physical recovery. Using placebos can improve healing.

Denial, therefore, as the first element of Kübler-Ross' model, actually assists in the healing process for the patient's recovery.

More so, denial assists the healthcare worker. Consider this list. Denial, in the form of a fighting spirit, hope, or faith promotes the following:

1. Healthcare professionals energize more when they refuse to believe that death is inescapable even when they are exhausted.

2. Denial in the form of hope propels professionals to try more options and be wisely experimental or diverse.

3. Denial that death is inevitable makes the professional be more diligent and attentive.

4. Denial that refuses to surrender to death, makes the healthcare worker act more aggressively in the care.

5. Denial that death is expected tends to motivate professionals to attend to more details carefully.

6. Denial in the form of hope and faith exudes a positive fighting spirit that is easily detected by the patient. This helps the patient mobilize the healing properties of hope and faith as well.

Value of Anger Toward Death's Prognosis

Anger can mobilize the warrior, fighting spirit, that benefits patients' recoveries as well. In like manner, your anger toward a patient's illness, plight, or injury can assist you if your anger is directed constructively. Anger, as a reaction to possible prognosis of death, can help you with the following:

1. Anger can motivate a tired and overworked medical professional to mobilize more actively and aggressively to save lives. Determination is triggered by anger constructively.

2. Anger which reacts to the "unfairness" of a patient's illness or plight can motivate professionals to intervene more diversely and creatively.

3. Anger can help practitioners be stubbornly persistent, a quality that also pushes the rest of the staff to try harder and not give-up.

4. Anger at the illness or injury of a patient can also stimulate a patient's will to live. This fighting spirit can pull patients from the grasps of death giving them a fighting chance.

Value of <u>Bargaining</u> as a Reaction to Decree of Death

Bargaining has helped many patients radically improve their bad habits and unhealthy neglect of their bodies. Diagnoses of cancer, kidney complications, diabetes, cardiac complications and many more have resulted in improved BMIs. Diagnoses motivate eating vegetables and fruits while avoiding saturated fats or processed preservatives. Exercise increases. Sleep improves. Meditation is practiced.

These are all proactive forms of bargaining with death.

"Will I get better if I ….?" is a question patient ask when they recognize that they need to take charge of their life to avoid death. Patients need to be the primary agents of their health.

In like manner, medical doctors and nurses who refuse to surrender to death's decree, will implement many changes in their practice. For example, doctors who claim to be atheist will begin to pray for a patient during tricky procedures. Doctors and nurses will plead with unconscious patients to "hang in there" even if they don't believe the patient can hear. Atypical procedures will be tried in desperate efforts to save a life. Doctor-patient or nurse-patient connections may become more intense after heroic successful efforts.

These are all forms of bargaining which medical professionals do when fighting against a likelihood of death.

"DO NOT GIVE UP! We are going to try something else," is the battle cry of bargaining. "Do not give up!" motivates an overworked medical team to become a collective power, fighting against death. It summons hope, faith, action, and energy.

Value of <u>Depression</u> When Treating Near-Death Patients

Kübler-Ross' stage of Depression is starkly different than Denial, Anger, and Bargaining because when depression is experienced, the fighting spirit and the active-agency is silenced. Instead, there is a slide into sad resolve, passive defeat, helplessness, and anguished loss of will to live.

When a healthcare worker slips into this phase of grief before the patient does, the patient will need to motivate the medical team. Conversely, when the patient and healthcare team synchronize into depression, some deeply intimate moments can be shared.

The grief of the patient can be beautifully empathized with, mirrored sincerely. Loss can be shared from the heart between two mortals who value life and share anguish about death. This honest rapport can support the "End of Life" experience. Grief shared also minimizes the burden of loss.

When medical staff can share this phase of grief together, the team changes. Emotional connection develops. Team spirit solidifies. Comradery flourishes. Authentic expressions of love are shared between the medical team, patients and their families. The burdened of death is shared.

It will be quite insensitive to say the following in the wrong setting. In the right setting, sharing sadness about losing a loved-one creates a collective value of life. There exists beauty when sharing deeply troubling moments. Ceremonies of life or moving funerals can stimulate resonance of love and purposefulness when depression synergizes the experience.

In depression, related to grief, death is faced boldly, potentially. In depression, death can be discussed honestly. In depression, empathy can be mirrored connectedly. In depression, a heartfelt celebration of life can be prepared (memorial services). In depression, human fragility and mortality is shared intimately. In depression, sitting together in palpable silence can link two who share love of life and sadness over loss.

When medical professionals navigate this phase of grief well, instead of avoiding depression, human connections and meaningfulness can flourish authentically. Please note, depression here is not clinically depression but rather the emotional experience of deep sadness.

Value of <u>Acceptance</u> by the Healthcare Worker for the Dying Patient

Acceptance is unlike any of the other phases of grief.

Agitated efforts settle down. Pain pauses. Peacefulness and quiet prevail for these moments of Acceptance. Pragmatic decisions are easier to make such as funeral arrangements, pain management, family farewell visits, financial provisions, and medical maintenance interventions.

During this phase of Acceptance, odd moments of laughter are shared. Memories are visited meaningfully. Forgiveness is asked and given. Broken bonds are mended. Future plans explored for those left behind. Fears, pains, and dashed hopes are discussed calmly. Faith is expressed or embraced at times too.

When the medical team also flows into these Acceptance moments with their patient, a type of harmony replaces worries and flurries of stressful efforts. Vigils begin, shared by the family and medical team.

The healing and calming aspects of the Acceptance phase cannot be experienced if death occurs in the midst of valiant medical interventions. Furthermore, the healing of acceptance cannot be mutual if the medical team, family and patient are not synchronized into this acceptance phase either.

Yet, when the patient, team and family are synchronized, a collective process occurs. The inevitability of everyone's death becomes a group recognition. All humans are mortal and fragile. We will all lose the battle against death. We share the moment of acceptance as peers, equals, and partners. We attempt to ease each other's pain of loss. Compassion returns as the main focus.

If Acceptance is mutually embraced prior to death, the healing of grief begins while the patient is alive. The belief that everyone did all they were equipped to do or knew to do has occurred.

Resolution is far better than unsettled feelings. It is tormenting to believe that more should have been done.

It is tormenting to believe someone died wrongfully as opposed to understandably. Regret breeds a painful guilt which we discuss in Chapter 10. Acceptance phase helps create resolution and assuage unwarranted guilt.

Summary and Self-Reflection

In this chapter, you are being asked to learn how to travel through your grief over your patients' deaths. You are asked to see grief reactions through new lenses.

You are being asked to see how meaningful each aspect of grief is. The phases of grief can motivate better medical interventions. Also rethink the importance of grief you experience when you extend compassion toward a patient who is facing death.

Again, for more wonderful help and tools, please go to the link below. Use the code **Recovery2020** to gain free access. It is a website designed for you and your team with respect for your work and thankfulness for your investment in patients' well-being.

abusetraumarecovery.com/healthcareworkerstraumarecovery

As with the other chapters, check off those items which now seem relevant to your professional experiences of death.

_____ 1. I now understand that compassion given to patients is part of the healing process. I understand it can be combined with medications and procedures beneficial for both me and the patient.

_____ 2. I now make a renewed commitment to experiencing and expressing genuine compassion to patients and their families.

_____ 3. I now recognize that I am NOT a good candidate for medical work that regularly deals with life and death moments or end-of-life experiences. I accept my limitations without shame or guilt.

_____ 4. I now recognize that I am a good candidate for medical work that involves regular life and death concerns and end-of-life issues for patients.

_____ 5. I understand the basic definition of all five phases of grief that were detailed by Kübler-Ross.

_____ 6. I understand that all of the five phases of grief can be reframed within my healthcare work to provide better care for my patients.

_____ 7. I understand that Denial, one of the phases of grief, can help patients and myself, implement interventions which could save lives.

_____ 8. I understand that Anger, another phase of grief, can be used to motivate interventions that could save lives.

_____ 9. I understand that Bargaining, another phase of grief, can be used to change certain patient and healthcare team behaviors that could save lives.

_____ 10. I understand that Depression, another phase of grief, can create empathic connections that may heal the patient or may help the transition to death be more thoughtfully managed.

_____ 11. I understand that feeling depression is different than becoming depressed in all aspects of my life.

_____ 12. I understand that empathy for another's plight is empathy for my own mortality as well but is not the same as me morning my own death.

_____ 13. I understand that feeling the presence of the patient's depression gives me the ability to be compassionate in ways that family members may not be able to share.

_____ 14. Shifting into Acceptance of my patients' inevitable death can breed different types of peace, kindness, and humanitarian efforts on my part.

_____ 15. Acceptance shared with my medical team can develop into mutual respect of our human frailty and commonality.

_____ 16. Experiencing the ebb and flow of each phase of grief with gentle awareness is something I wish to practice. Chapter 9 discusses these tools more.

_____ 17. I will check out the audio meditations that correspond with this chapter at abusetraumarecovery.com/healthcareworkerstraumareco very and use the code **Recovery2020** to access such freely.

Chapter 9
More Tools to Manage Grief

Practice

The key word for this chapter is PRACTICE.

You will practice compassion with yourself, your team, and your patients.

You will practice allowing the phases of grief to ebb and flow through you without grief owning every aspect of your life nor dominating all your relationships, thoughts, and feelings.

You will practice transitioning from one aspect of your personality into other parts of your personality so that you can be present both with yourself and with those you help.

You will practice replacing necessary stressful responses and necessary emergency urgency with ease, calm, and homelife enjoyments.

You will practice being a complex human being who can manage shifting through complex human experiences without losing your core identity.

You will practice being a healthy and evolving human being who is flexible, adaptable, and respectful of yourself and others.

Physical Practice

Ideally, every hour at work you should take a two to five minute break to stretch, breathe deeply, jog in place or create a quick sweat.

Ideally, hourly you would drink refreshing water to keep hydrated and help your organs functions.

Ideally, you would eat healthy living foods that gave you energy to burn and nutrients to support your body's extra needs during stressful medical work.

Ideally, you would sleep soundly and long enough to fully refresh your brain's functions and your body's regulatory systems.

Chapter 3 very specifically guides you through these practices which will greatly support your physiological functions that will help you minimize the negative impact of grief and death's stressfulness.

Also, use the code **Recovery2020** to gain free access to the **Healthcare Workers Trauma Recovery Courses**. The link to the courses specific to your physical health is:

https://abusetraumarecovery.com/courses/course-3-trauma-recovery-and-your-physical-health/

Furthermore, Yoga Master Adrienne is sharing 6 of her yoga videos with you that specifically deal with trauma release. They are short and deliciously refreshing. Here is that link too:

https://abusetraumarecovery.com/courses/course-4-yoga-for-recovery-body-mind-soul/

Self-Care Practice

Emotional self-care enables you to feel emotions fluidly without becoming rigidly attached to emotions even when they are intense. Understanding that grief, for example, is a fluid process that shifts from one emotion to another helps you endure and watch how you are shifting. Shifting fluidly from one set of behaviors to other emotions helps you realize that you are not a rigid robot that only has one function button.

Emotions are not to be owned. Emotions are not to be used as identifiers. Emotions are fluid, ever changing reactions that correspond with external moments and events sometimes or internal thoughts or interpretations sometimes. Emotions are like water. Water changes structure with the temperature. Water can be contained inside a glass but can also spill randomly. Water can ease, cleanse or erode. Water is variable and so are emotions.

Too often people own their emotions as if they are personality definitions. For example, "I'm an anxious person." "I'm a depressive." "You're such an angry person all the time." These are erroneous statements. No person is always anxious, nor always depressed nor always angry. These emotions are transitory. They intermixed with other emotions that come and go as well. They are reactive, like a barometer reading air pressure.

So, let your emotions flow. Let them come and go and shift. You can honor them by understanding their message. You can honor them by responding positively to any needs they express. But do not let them own your identity. Do not let them control your thoughts. Do not let them dictate all your actions. Do not let them determine your decisions. Emotions are meant to inform, but not decide. Emotions are meant to help you connect or disconnect but not replace judicious choices about who or when to do so.

Taking a shower after a sweaty workout or busy shift is meant to cleanse and refresh. In like manner allow your emotions to flow through you. As much as possible use your emotions to inform you. When anxious, fatigued or cranky, its likely time to refresh your energies. When furious, offended, or depressed, it may be time to cleanse your circumstances.

Again, use **Recovery2020** as the code to access all the Online Courses at AbuseTraumaRecovery.com. One course in particular teaches more about navigating your emotions during recovery. Here is that link:

https://abusetraumarecovery.com/courses/navigating-emotions-during-recovery/

Practice Inner Peace

Perhaps for you, fluid emotional responses to intense work will be helped by practicing Inner Peaceful Moments or Zen Zone moments. Review Chapter 4 and select four Inner Peaceful practices from the hundreds mentioned. Chapters 4, 5, & 6 in this book are also designed to help you relearn to manage your daily life attentively and kindly toward yourself. Also, use **Recovery2020** to gain access to the *Inner Peaceful Courses* which contain 14+ quick and effective audios that you can listen to from your phone during your brief breaks at work. You will find your favorite audios will have impact on you quickly and will teach you to ESCAPE.

ESCAPE Practice

While at work, commit to three to ten minutes every hour or every three hours to ESCAPE.

1. **E**motionally refresh
2. **S**oothe racing thoughts
3. **C**alm physical jitters
4. **A**ccept troubling events as experiences
5. **P**ractice Inner Peace
6. **E**ase back into your core values of respecting yourself and others (Chapter 11)

ESCAPE every hour, if possible. Bathroom breaks. Water breaks. Exercise breaks. Socializing beaks. Eating breaks. These breaks are essential for you in order to regulate your physiological reactivity to stress and tragedy. These important ESCAPE breaks regulate your emotional and mental reactivity as well. Break-up your STS or trauma reactivity cycle often.

Here is the link to the Inner Peaceful Moments of ESCAPE. Each Class has two or more Zen Zone moments of ESCAPE for you to practice. Choose your favorites. Pass these links on to your team too.

https://abusetraumarecovery.com/courses/course-6-create-your-inner-peace/

ESCAPE Doing Daily Dreary Chores

Accomplishing dreary dull chores of your homelife can actually help you ESCAPE and transition back into your other nonhealthcare existence. Those dishes may look terribly dirty and easy to ignore but they can also provide you 10-minutes of doing nonurgent, nonemergency-oriented activities. Listen to pleasant music, whatever is your style, or podcasts during the dirty simple deeds. Enjoy your glass of whatever while sweeping your floor. Dance a playful jig while taking trash out. Giggle and laugh with friends who understand that jokes free you, and silly stories ease the day while cleaning the tub.

Chapter 5 explores many ways to reorganize your daily life too. Let your NORMAL nonwork life become pleasantly normalized. Again, use **Recovery2020** for yet another set of wonderful videos, journaling moments and audios that will walk you through this practice as well. Here is the link about daily chores:

https://abusetraumarecovery.com/courses/course-5-reorganizing-daily-chores-of-life/

Retreat Practice

ESCAPE by retreating frequently. Retreat with friends and family to have fun times with games, activities, and laughter. Retreat with entertainment that helps you regroup and recharge. Retreat into movement that lets your body release tension and breathe fully. Retreat into ESCAPE novels, stories, or shallow tales. Retreat into spiritual practices that enlighten or peaceful practices that ease.

For spiritual practices that enlighten, consider creating art, gardening, singing or reading a few of the chapters in *Your Soaring Phoenix*

(link: https://www.amazon.com/Your-Soaring-Phoenix-Spiritual-Ascension-ebook/dp/B00KMNFU46/ref=sr_1_1?dchild=1&keywords=Your+Soaring+Phoenix+by+Dr.+Carol+Francis&qid=1593473559&sr=8-1)

For your peaceful retreats consider reading poetry, lyrics, short stories or *Own Your Peace: KISS Method for Inner Peaceful Living*

(link: https://www.amazon.com/Your-Soaring-Phoenix-Spiritual-Ascension-ebook/dp/B00KMNFU46/ref=sr_1_1?dchild=1&keywords=Your+Soaring+Phoenix+by+Dr.+Carol+Francis&qid=1593473559&sr=8-1)

Social Practice

Socialize in ways that do not replicate your work life arena. If you love socializing with friends from work, do so and contract with everyone to NOT discuss work when you need to be laughing, moving, goofing, creating, and smiling together. Seriously, ESCAPE.

Meditation, Mindfulness, Self-Hypnosis

For some of you, meditation and mindfulness practices through apps such as CALM, HEADSPACE or Mindvalley apps perfectly help you ESCAPE. Transcendental meditation, Yoga practices, Shamanic Journeying my suit you well.

For others, these practices are too passive. They perhaps will not distract you enough from your racing thoughts, intense concerns, or traumatic physiological revving. You might consider using the BrainTap device and its protocols to gain refreshing 20 minutes of meditative relief. Other such devices are discussed in Chapter 6 or demonstrated at this link:

https://abusetraumarecovery.com/courses/course-7-self-therapy-moments/

Remember, choose what works for you that helps you ESCAPE in healthy and authentic ways. Live your life, your style, your way effectively.

Checklist of Tools Offered in Chapter 9

Check off those items which match you today.

_____ 1. I will implement two to four of the Practices suggested in this chapter that match my personality and match how I ESCAPE.

_____ 2. I will practice some those two to four choices many times during the day for 3-10 minutes.

_____ 3. I will practice some of those two to four choices several times a week and practice the ESCAPE processes which work for me until I can easily capture my personal experience of peace, ease, normalcy.

_____ 4. I will practice those choices that refresh my body, emotions, and thoughts. If I chose items that do not seem to be helping within 7 days, I will select other tools to practice.

_____ 5. I will respect myself enough to learn to fluidly feel my emotions while at work and fluidly ESCAPE troubling emotions and thoughts when I leave my work behind.

_____ 6. I understand the need to create moments of ESCAPE as such will break the physiological cycle that fuels my body's trauma responses, my STS response.

_____ 7. I understand the need to practice moments of ESCAPE since such will interrupt STS reactive emotions, thoughts and behaviors that are related to my trauma work experiences.

_____ 8. I will respect my unique styles and will ESCAPE in ways that work for me and ESCAPE in ways that are healthy for me as well.

_____ 9. I will look through this chapter and explore the links to videos, audios, and journal exercises which might be very helpful at:

https://abusetraumarecovery.com/healthcareworkerstrau marecovery/

_____10. I will use and share this code **Recovery2020** so that I and my medical team, even my family, can practice moving away from the horrible impact of trauma work and practice being fluidly adaptable in all aspects of my life. Here is the website link again to share with others: https://abusetraumarecovery.com/healthcareworkerstrau marecovery/

Chapter 10
Managing Your Fatal Mistake

We now will discuss a taboo topic.

This is taboo at least for medical professionals who fear malpractice lawsuits, dismissal from employment, slander, and loss of license to practice.

What is this taboo? Admitting that you made a fatal mistake within your medical practice.

This chapter may not yet apply to some of you. You may not have had this experience, yet. Nonetheless, it might help you understand others or help prevent you from destructively reacting to this type of event when it happens to you.

Between you and me, I know you are human, and human mistakes are fairly typical. I will assume that you are a caring person who would always wish to provide medical care with precision and calm accuracy. I know, however, that you have made mistakes you do not even recognize. I know you have made mistakes you have learned from and will always avoid in the future. You will make more mistakes in your future too. This is a probability even a prediction, because you are human.

I know that it is likely you made mistakes from which your patients easily could recover. I suspect you have also made some mistakes you worry (or definitely know) have been fatal to your patients.

If you are a caring individual and a conscientious professional, you absolutely will be riddled with guilt and worry about the potentially fatal mistake(s) you made. You may also worry about making such mistakes in your future. Medical treatments are very complicated, and options are plentiful; therefore, anyone human is likely to make mistakes.

- Erroneous decisions
- Incomplete history taking
- Pharmaceutical mishaps
- Ignorance about conditions
- Ignorance about treatments
- Lack of experience with procedures and equipment
- Failure to attend to important details
- Details your mentors failed to teach or you failed to study

Making mistakes is a painful probability to live with. Yet, the more you care about doing right by your patients, the more you must admit that making mistakes can and do occur. These mistakes need to be caught quickly. As a consequence, you need to be fluidly able to admit when mistakes happen that can be quickly reversed. You need to be ready to intervene as quickly as possible instead of denying you made a mistake that could still be corrected in time.

Fatal mistakes can of course not be corrected. The patient has died. Perhaps your fatal mistake caused the death. Perhaps the patient would have died regardless of your mistake. Either way, you may opt to tell the authorities and supervisors about your mistake or admit such to your patient's family. However, you may also opt to keep such admissions secret. Harboring such secrets creates tremendous internal tension, guilt, and self-reproach.

Suicide is high among doctors, especially doctors who treat risky life and death conditions. Perhaps, some of those suicides have extended from the internal pains of knowing about these fatal mistakes and keeping them secret.

Truly, *we don't want doctors and nurses to commit suicide*. We want to deal with any emotional torments and internal secrets that befuddle healthcare workers so that suicidal thoughts will not be enacted.

157

Perhaps the first step is to admit to yourself that you might have made or absolutely did make a fatal mistake in your medical practice. Second, admit to yourself that you feel devastated by your error and the life it may have lost.

Third, explore if your secret will be used for good or will it be used to harm you and others in the future. What does this mean? All humans must learn from their mistakes if they are to evolve. If a fatal mistake can teach those who practice medicine not to make that fatal mistake in the future, then some good comes from this horrible moment. If a fatal mistake can be used to teach others to avoid such carelessness or shortsightedness, then some good comes.

If you as a medical professional can be more loving, more humble, more kind toward patients and co-workers some good has developed. If you can be more thoughtful about how you work under stress and guard against stress-related mistakes, some good has come. If you are now more careful to avoid activities which led up to the mistake (sleeplessness, alcohol, drugs, conflicts, arrogance, ignorance) then some good can evolve from the mistake.

While you may be able to help the dying live, you are not God. You are not omniscient, not omnipresent, and not omni-anything. You are a mere human being who engages in very serious work that may save lives. Because you work in such risky situations, you are also likely to have flawed judgement at times. You will have inadequate knowledge and experience because you are limited as a human. You will lack foresight at times and misstep somehow that might be fatal. Ideally, we could learn all we needed to learn without ever making a mistake but that ideal is NOT reality.

The heightened probability of making a fatal mistake comes with the territory of working in risky life and death arenas. Yes, you are always cautioned to be careful and precise. Yes, you are human and imperfect as well.

You and I are having this discussion about your imperfections and your mistakes because you will need to navigate living your life fully and helpfully irrespective of your imperfections.

These are common reactions to keeping this type of secret:

Guilt
Shame
Embarrassment
Fear of being discovered
Reckless and artificial arrogance
Self-sabotaging behaviors
Unhealthy escapes through drugs and alcohol
Passive-aggressive projections onto others
Destruction to relationships
Severe self-reproach that becomes self-harming
Self-punishment which takes many forms
Chronic antagonistic thoughts drowning you mentally
Chronic horrific emotions creating chaos or torment

Sudden abandonment of career
Becoming homeless
Suicide

If any of these are relevant to you, let's talk. I can't tell you if it is right to tell the authorities, supervisors, or family members. It might be best if you do. It might not be best. Your circumstances are complex. You have to come to terms with that yourself. I'd suggest discussing such with a wise therapist or priest. I also can't tell you how you can live with yourself if you do tell or do not to tell.

I, however, would like to suggest to you that any of these strong reactions I listed above need to be converted into reactions that are healthy for you, healthy for your family and friends, and healthy for your future patients and their families.

Recognize for a moment that not one of your medical colleagues will finish their career without at least one very serious mistake that may have cost someone's life. Not one. Their stories remain unspoken. Their secret also is kept hidden. Your profession does not encourage such revealing disclosures.

Please know though, you are not alone.

Recognize too that you might be able to be more evolved, more educated, more humble, more experienced as a medical professional than you were before recognizing your mistake. In other words, it is possible you can now be a better nurse, a better doctor, a better healthcare professional now that you know you are vulnerable to making serious mistakes.

Can you be better at your work than you were before? If so, perhaps many patients will benefit from your learning moment. Can you benefit others now that you have learned? If so, consider doing so. Make the commitment to be wiser, kinder, more educated. Make a commitment to work with a team that catches each other's potential errors without being stupidly offended by each other's corrections.

Learn from your mistake and pass your newly found wisdom forward to benefit many others.

Almost every wartime deployed soldier has nightmares about who they killed even when told to defend and protect. Too many soldiers commit suicide over such dreaded memories. We lose their expertise, their compassion, and their wisdom when they commit suicide. We don't want to lose your expertise, compassion and wisdom that was earned at great cost.

Become recommitted to excellence in your healthcare work.

Use your mistake to be better than what you were before. Recognize your vulnerability to making mistakes. Have greater patience and compassion while you help others navigate their mistakes too.

Rise above your guilt, shame, and chagrin to be a better human being and medical professional in order to pay your debt forward. Let someone else, many others in fact, benefit from your very tough learning experience.

Don't bury your head and deny your secret to yourself. Instead use that self-awareness and create as much good out of that moment as you possibly can.

Nightmares are born from regrets, deep regrets, sometimes.

On the other hand, great humanitarian movements, organizations, and gifts are also birthed out of deep regrets.

I am pained for you that you had this mistake that hangs over your head and pulls you down in your heart.

I plead with you to use this mistake for good.

Create the Good your mistake can generate. And as you read the next and last chapter, be sure to also

Create Respect.

Chapter 11
CREATE RESPECT

Traumatic events force us to face our frailties. Our limitations vex us. Our mortality frightens us. We grieve we could not do more. We worry we failed to do something we should have done. We fret we won't be able to rise to the next demanding moments.

Guilt swallows us.
Shame confuses us.
Hopelessness deflates us.

During emergencies, we care to do our best. Yet, we know our best may not save the lives of those who depend upon us. Weight of conflicting responsibilities drowns us. Impossible dilemmas defeat us. Grievous moments haunt us. Loneliness of death, suffering, and loss plagues us.

I don't need to tell you stories from Emergency Rooms, Nursing Homes, Skilled-Nursing Facilities, Urgent Care Centers, ICUs, Ambulances, Disaster Sites, Covid19 Hospital Floors, et cetera. You have lived those moments. You have helped in those places. You now need to recover after helping others during their ordeals.

Feeling demoralized, helpless, limited, defeated are natural post-traumatic reactions that can lead to more severe depression, lethargy, or hopelessness. These understandable reactions can also lead to panic attacks, social isolation, general anxiety, and phobias.

In this book, we offer tools that will assist you in your recovery in hopes that your PTSD, or STS, or Compassion Fatigue, or Professional Burnout will not defeat you. We have spent less time empathizing with your painful memories. Less time warning you about the adverse impact of trauma work. We have given little attention to your very understandable and common reactions to the trauma work which you might have suffered.

Instead, I wanted to spend more time providing you some tools that would help you remember who you can be and help you shift into being a renewed you. We want you once again to become –

Celebratory for your successes and triumphs
Realistic about losses, failures and mistakes
Easy with yourself and others when easiness soothes
Accepting of your human limitations and failures
Tenacious even when success seems farfetched
Enthusiastic about your ability to recover fully

*R*espectful for your efforts to be helpful
*E*nergetically growing your health, peace, and loves
*S*ympathetic toward others' losses, confusions, and fears
*P*urposeful when enriching your mind and skills
*E*arnest about connecting with worthy people in your life
*C*ompassionate when you simply cannot do more
*T*ough when grit and resilience need to be activated

Notice the first letter of these 13 injunctions above spells out CREATE RESPECT. At all moments during your recovery, remember this injunction – CREATE RESPECT for yourself, your skills, your efforts and your recovery needs. CREATE RESPECT for the time, space, and tools that will help you regroup.

This book began by urging you to Respect your own style of recovery. We wish to end this self-help book with the same instructions. CREATE RESPECT for yourself especially since you understand that healing takes time, tools, wisdom, and compassion.

CREATE RESPECT daily for yourself as a skilled professional who tenaciously attempts to save others against impossible odds under adverse conditions.

Please CREATE RESPECT for yourself related to the sacrifices you make, the risks you take, and the horrors you endure.

Please CREATE RESPECT for yourself as you forgive yourself for errors or limitations. Be gracious toward your awkwardness or ignorance. Be understanding of your outbursts of anxiety and expressions of righteous anger. Be easy on yourself as you reflect upon what you didn't do but now wish you could have done.

You did much more than most. You tried much harder than many. You showed-up more than you wanted to risk or sacrifice. CREATE RESPECT for all your efforts, big and small.

Please CREATE RESPECT as you take your time to recover all the aspects of yourself which need to rest, reset, recalibrate, renew, retrain, and refresh.

I wrote this book to express my RESPECT for who you are: your skills, your emotional compassion, your mental toughness, your physical endurance, and your spiritual commitment.

I also wrote this book because I want you to CREATE RESPECT daily for your limitations as a human being who needs time and space to recuperate physically, regroup mentally, reconfigure emotionally, and rediscover spiritually.

Thank you for letting me help you.

Do not hesitate to reach out to myself and my team for further assistance at TherapyCounselingCoaching.com.

Please avail yourself of the resources I have created for you as often as needed at:

AbuseTraumaRecovery.com/HealthCareWorkersTraumaRecovery.

I will be thinking and caring about you for the rest of my life. I will be grateful that your team of Health Care Workers has saved my life, saved my family members' lives, and saved the lives of many I have known and loved and those I have not yet met.

Thank you.
Very Respectfully Yours,
Dr. Carol Francis

About the Author

Dr. Carol Francis, for over forty years, has helped survivors recover their verve and empowerment after traumatic experiences. She is a Licensed Clinical Psychologist, Licensed Marriage, Family and Child Therapist, Certified Hypnotherapist, and Trauma Specialist practicing in the Los Angeles Beach Cities.

Dr. Carol Francis has authored 19 books, available on Amazon or at DrCarolFrancis.com. Her comprehensive online Courses, Blogs, and Vlogs are offered at AbuseTraumaRecovery.com for survivors, professionals, and families. Dr. Carol Francis lives in Southern California with her family, animals, and nightly breathtaking sunsets shared with friends. Weekly, she interviews fascinating authors and professionals on her podcast, "Dr. Carol Francis" or "Make Life Happen." Her trauma-related books include:

Schizoid Anxiety

Helping Children After Natural Disasters

Helping Children Through Divorce

Reintegrating Soldiers with Families

Evolving Women's Consciousness

Own Your Peace

Your Soaring Phoenix

Paths to Recovery After Abuse and Trauma

Recovery After Trauma Work